MYSTER

A THEOLOGY OF CHURCH

CHARLES HILL

GILL AND MACMILLAN

Published in Ireland by
Gill and Macmillan Ltd
Goldenbridge
Dublin 8
with associated companies in
Auckland, Delhi, Gaborone, Hamburg, Harare,
Hong Kong, Johannesburg, Kuala Lumpur, Lagos, London,
Manzini, Melbourne, Mexico City, Nairobi,
New York, Singapore, Tokyo

First published 1990 by Collins Dove, Victoria
0 7171 1893 2
Printed in Australia

The cover reproduces the twelfth century mosaic in the apse of the basilica of San Clemente in Rome. Its theme is the cross as the tree of life, reminiscent of that tree which grew in the garden of Eden (*Genesis* 2:9, 24). The artist depicts the cross standing between heaven and earth, and bringing life to all. The mosaic can remind us of the Church as mystery of life within God's whole plan to bring life to all things through the Paschal Mystery of Jesus.

Nihil Obstat: Rev. Peter J. Kenny, D.D.,
Diocesan Censor
Imprimatur: Hilton F. Deakin, Ph.D.,
Vicar General
Date: 4th September, 1990

The Nihil Obstat and Imprimatur are official declarations that a book or pamphlet is free of doctrinal or moral error. No implication is contained therein that those who have granted the Nihil Obstat and Imprimatur agree with the contents, opinions or statements expressed. They do not necessarily signify that the work is approved as a basic text for catechetical instruction.

To my local church of Lower Mountains NSW
in the hope that the mystery of life
will become a reality also for us.

CONTENTS

INTRODUCTION

'At a certain state of crisis or point of maturation, one particular mystery—one particular part of the unique whole—comes, as it were, into the foreground of the reflective landscape.'[1] Thus wrote that great French theologian Henri De Lubac in the years before the Second Vatican Council, at the midpoint of this century. 'As far as the development of doctrine is concerned, the twentieth century is destined to be "the century of the Church".'

The century of the Church

Prophetic words. The Catholic community in particular had just emerged from centuries of confinement within an institutional model of Church; they had begun again—after the false start of Modernism and its aftermath—to wrestle with the critical challenges of biblical scholarship and post-Enlightenment investigation generally. Pope Pius XII had cleared the way for an examination of the scriptural data on Church with his charter for biblical scholars, *Divino Afflante Spiritu*,[2] and his own endorsement of a biblical figure of Church in *Mystici Corporis Christi*,[3] both encyclicals appearing in 1943.

Even if this option for one New Testament figure of Church had the effect of foreshortening the perspective of Church for some ecclesiologists, there were others who took heart from the former encyclical to consider the whole of the biblical tradition, even if some, including De Lubac himself, would suffer for their adventurous spirit. Studies would appear (not only by Catholics, of course) on the huge range of biblical figures, images, models of Church. Pius XII, a most magisterial pontiff, would also place a healthy accent on another tradition of the community, liturgical tradition, in the 1947 encyclical *Mediator Dei*.[4] This document kept Church at the focus of attention, and also acknowledged the need to consider Eastern as well as Western practice and theology.

If the climate after *Humani Generis*[5] of 1950 did not promote the Church's self-examination to the same extent, such awareness was promoted by John XXIII's decision in 1959 to summon a Church Council a century after Vatican I. Preparatory commissions placed the Church at the forefront of attention, and, after some hesitation, utilised the wider acquaintance with biblical and patristic data and the theological investigations of Church carried on by theologians of the calibre of De Lubac and Yves Congar. The Constitution on the Church, entitled significantly *Lumen Gentium*[6] after the reference in *Isaiah* 42:6 to the missionary role of the Suffering Servant, was proclaimed as the cornerstone of the Council in 1964, the same year that Paul VI released his own endorsement of this theme in his first encyclical *Ecclesiam Suam*.[7] Other Council documents built on and acknowledged the Constitution. Such pronouncements on the Church paralleled similar contemporary investigations by other Christian communities, particularly the Orthodox community and the World Council of Churches. The twentieth was certainly proving to be 'the century of the Church'.

Two decades after Vatican II, a rich period for theological writing on Church, a special Synod of Bishops considered the condition of the Catholic community in the intervening period and, as we shall see, had their own views on how Church should now be seen. Their *Final Report*[8] suggested some developments had gone far enough. But it was the meaning of Church that continued to fascinate; even the 1987 Synod on the laity considered this subject within a theology of Church as the vine and its branches, as appears from John Paul II's post-synodal apostolic exhortation *Christifideles Laici*.[9] The 1990 Synod is directed to the study of those ordained to ministry in the Church. In these postconciliar years too, the Catholic community was conducting dialogue on Church with the Anglican Community (through ARCIC, the Anglican-Roman Catholic International Commission), the Orthodox, and various Protestant communities.

A new Church for a new century

So the prophecy had come to pass: the twentieth century has proved to be 'the century of the Church'—at least as far as multiplicity of magisterial statements and diversity of theologies are concerned. There is certainly a richness and pluriformity in theologising about Church; theologians no longer feel inhibited by one model or figure, biblical or societal. Yet one wonders if Christians have profited significantly in their lives and thinking from this attention to Church at another level. For many contemporary Christians, even though the Church may be a preoccupation, it is not a subject they relish. Catholics at any rate, while ready enough to expose a personal history of vexations and disillusionment in their dealings with churchmen and churchwomen, do not come readily to courses and study sessions on the Church—it is not an attractive subject for them. They are evidently not enjoying the beauty of the vision of Church that the Scriptures and Christian tradition can offer them. Their experience is otherwise.

In addition, Providence is intervening to change the shape of the Church they are accustomed to. Whatever the health of the Church in the postcommunist era in Eastern Europe, numerically the mainstream churches in the developed countries are declining. There is a call for the refounding of the Church, on the model perhaps of the more vigorous Third Church. If the twentieth has been the century of the Church in theologising and magisterial statement, the twenty first will need to be the century of the new Church, in life and practice.

Providence, the passage of time, the irreversibility of present trends—call it what you will—will ensure that the Church of the third millennium will not be what we have grown up to accept as the norm. It would surely accord with Providence if we could divine a theology of Church suited to these providential developments and capable of contributing to them. Not that we are short on theologies of Church, as we have seen. One theologian admits 'a crisis of images', claiming that we have passed rapidly from one image or figure or model to another in a way that has only unsettled the faithful. It has not been so easy to discern what is adequate and fundamental in our understanding of Church as far as Christian tradition presents it, and how this understanding of Church relates to the teaching of Jesus and the plan that God has created for all, even beyond the Church. Beyond the dazzling range of images and models that have replaced Bellarmine's monolith, we certainly need to appreciate the mystery of the Church, a mystery of life (*communio, koinonia* in the language of recent magisterial— if ancient biblical—insights), a life to be accepted and lived.

A theology for a new Church

Is this not just one more theology of Church, to add to the confusion? The reader can turn to the following pages to see how an understanding of Church in these terms gets beyond the figures to the reality beneath. At any rate, pending acceptance of the argument developed in these pages, it is possible to set some requirements for a theology of Church that meets contemporary needs. It will have to be a *traditional* theology in the sense of one responsive to the ways in which the Christian community has transmitted its foundational experiences to us; we are clearly in the hands of Providence, and we must listen to that community telling us of God's revelatory, saving dealings with them from the beginning. Our theology of Church will arise from an appreciation of biblical tradition—the whole Bible, not some personal, partial canon. It will also necessitate an appreciation of patristic tradition, those many centuries of reflection on the mystery of Christ by great spokespersons, teachers, scholars and catechists, though these are often ignored today, even in seminary formation, but treasured and conned by great moderns like Meyendorff and Staniloae, De Lubac and Congar. We will also need an understanding of dogmatic tradition—those statements of the hierarchical magisterium which themselves attempt to mediate to us a reflection on those other forms of tradition.

It will have to be a *completely Christian* theology, one

that takes account of the whole of Christian tradition, not simply that of the West, let alone one segment of Western Christianity. We need to imitate the sensitivity of Paul VI embracing Patriarch Athenagoras and speaking of our 'sister churches' of East and West, and his reconciliation with Pope Shenouda of Alexandria, spiritual leader of the Orthodox Coptic church, admitting that fifteen centuries of division were due simply to misunderstanding of terminology. We need to listen as well to the other followers of Jesus the Christ, and particularly the agreed statements on Church that come from our continuing dialogue with Anglicans, Lutherans, Baptists and others. The Catholic community thus openly acknowledges that it has no monopoly on experience and thinking of Church, though not all theologies admit as much.

Our theology of Church will thus be healthily ecumenical. To be truly *universal*, however, it will have to situate the Church within the whole of the mystery of Christ, God's plan for all that he has created, the material world as well as the people within it. This does not arise out of any passing fad about ecology or conservation in order to placate the 'greenies'. Our study of biblical tradition will highlight in particular the full dimensions of God's plan and Jesus' message on the 'kingdom', and also the relevance of worldly concerns to the Christian calling. So many theological systems leave Church and world at odds, and thus also leave Christians at a loss when it comes to seeing life as an integrated whole—despite the clear message of some of the biblical writings, an understanding which is conveniently, but disastrously, omitted by some theologians. A sound theology of Church will give a recipe for life in the world—provided the Church is seen in the context of the mystery of Christ.

Hence the accent in this book whose title emphasises the Church as mystery, as God's plan to bring life. That is the reality that underlies, and in fact requires, the range of figures, images and models of the Church. It is a plan that had Paul gasping in wonderment, 'O the depth of the riches and wisdom and knowledge of God', after three chapters (9–11) in *Romans* pondering only one aspect of it—the joint share in it by Gentiles and his fellow Jews. The reality offers many more aspects than that, as Paul also came to realise, so that the mystery (in his sense and ours) is no mere puzzle but a vast sacred reality—not something unintelligible but something of 'inexhaustible intelligibility', as one modern theologian puts it. Because that is not our usual sense of the word in modern English, and because theological and magisterial statement is not always consistent either, the task of educating in these terms is not a simple one; but it is an urgent task if Church is to be adequately understood.

That is my deep conviction, and the evidence assembled in the following pages supports it. The theology of Church developed here, on those traditional lines, will call for some adjustment to our thinking. It is thus not a book for beginners, though biblical and patristic evidence is usually luminously clear. In case some terminology is not immediately familiar, a glossary is appended for ready reference. On the other hand, this is not a specialist work; scholarly detail has been kept to a minimum and as far as possible out of sight. I would, however, suggest to the specialists that an acknowledgement of mystery in ecclesiology is overdue. As a mystery of life, Church is to be lived, not simply pondered; at the end of these chapters some points are raised for discussion with a view to practical application of the theology. If, as in St Augustine's beautiful definition, 'the Church consists of fellowship of the whole world,'[10] what better thing to share with one another than our believing and theologising about Church.

Part of the first chapter appeared in *Compass Theology Review* 23 (Autumn 1989), and acknowledgement is made here of permission to reprint it.

Charles Hill,
Australian Catholic University, Sydney

1
THE CHURCH AS MYSTERY

In its issue of December 6, 1985, the German newspaper *Die Zeit* headed up its assessment of the recently concluded Extraordinary Synod of Bishops in Rome with this one-liner: 'Flight into mystery'.[1] The Synod, 'extraordinary' in the sense of interrupting the series of meetings at three-yearly intervals begun by Vatican II in recognition of the rarity of general councils, had been studying the impact of that Council a quarter-century on. *Die Zeit* thus correctly identified one of the bishops' key theological motifs in their *Final Report*.[2] It was also one of the German bishops' particular concerns in their addresses to the Synod. Similarly, it was not wide of the mark in implying that choice of this motif represented a re-direction of thinking for some Synodal participants. The journalist and these participants, however, were perhaps unaware that the direction of the Synod's *Final Report*[3] in presenting the Church as mystery was not a novelty when compared with the Council's own thinking on Church.

Inadequate notion of mystery

Still, the implication was there that the Synod bishops were reacting with alarm to unfavourable trends, and were taking refuge in some haven when they chose this notion to represent the Church to the Catholic community of the last quarter of the twentieth century. For them the term mystery represented an inward movement, away from the worldly context of Church life towards a spiritual core. Claiming the support of Vatican II's Constitution on the Church, the Synod bishops in their *Message to the People of God*, which was also released at the close of the Synod, said:

> We are aware that the Church cannot renew herself unless this spiritual note of mystery is more deeply

rooted in the hearts of Christians. This note has as its first characteristic element the universal call to holiness which is addressed to all the faithful as well as to those who, according to their state in life, follow the evangelical counsels. The innermost reality of the Church must be understood in this way if we are to avoid false sociological or political interpretations of the nature of the Church.[4]

We can examine later the bishops' motivation in adopting this stance in the light of the quarter century since the Council. The fact is that their choice—a most happy choice in our view—could be interpreted as a flight, a retreat, because of references to the 'spiritual note of mystery... the innermost reality of the Church,'[5] as though 'mystery' was meant in this sense.

There was, of course, and always will be, plenty of encouragement for people to use the word mystery in this inadequate sense (even outside Agatha Christie's detective novels); for it is, at least in reference to the Church, an inadequate sense, despite being used frequently, even in solemn magisterial statements. Pope Paul VI often spoke of the Church as *a* mystery, implying at times that it thus lay beyond our understanding, like other mysteries of religion. 'It can never claim to be sufficiently investigated and understood.' he wrote in 1964 during the Council in his first encyclical, *Ecclesiam Suam*. He then went on to quote St Paul's use of the word mystery in this sense, though in fact it is Paul's thinking, as we shall see, which provides the basis for the much more adequate sense: 'For it contains "the publication of a mystery kept hidden from the beginning of time,"'[6] referring to *Eph* 3:9. There are countless theological texts dealing with the mysteries of religion that employ the word in the less adequate sense, including Matthias Scheeben's famous manual, *The Mysteries of Christianity*:

Christianity entered the world as a religion replete with mysteries. It was proclaimed as the mystery of Christ (*Rom* 16:25–27; *Col* 1:25–27), as the 'mystery of the kingdom of God' (*Mk* 4:11; *Lk* 8:10). Its ideas and doctrines were unknown, unprecedented; and they

> were to remain inscrutable and unfathomable.[7]

(It is particularly ironic that Scheeben, in addition to misinterpreting Paul's usage, also refers to that single illuminating occurrence of mystery in the Gospels at *Mk* 4:11 that declares God's 'kingdom' (in Jesus) to be the mystery, the vast sacred reality, as we shall investigate later.) More recent textbooks, like Andrew Greeley's *The Great Mysteries: An Essential Catechism*, show a willingness to admit the more adequate sense, but without complete success:

> By 'mystery' I do not mean something that is hard to cope with because it is obscure and baffling; I mean something that is hard to cope with because it is so bright and dazzling...
> The Greek word from which 'symbol' and 'mystery' come can also be translated as 'secret'. St Paul is frequently translated as speaking of the great 'secret' hidden from the ages and revealed in the Lord Jesus.[8]

(That inadequate choice of 'secret' appears in some versions of the Pauline passages, such as the New English Bible.)

A more influential, but still deficient, presentation of the Church as mystery has been Avery Dulles's *Models of the Church*, where Dulles sees 'the mysterious character of the Church' as the grounds for developing a series of models 'to illuminate the mysteries of faith'—in this case the Church. Dulles sees even Vatican II's reference to the mystery of the Church as implying 'that the Church is not fully intelligible to the finite mind of man,' and relates this to the apophatic tradition in theology which proceeds by way of elimination rather than exposition.[9] Vatican II, however, in speaking of the Church as mystery, meant much more than that, as we shall see.

We associate the apophatic tradition in ecclesiology, as in theology generally, with Orthodox theologians in particular. From patristic times the East has always accentuated divine transcendence. So it is no surprise to find this limited sense of mystery in the Romanian theologian Dumitru Staniloae writing recently on 'The mystery of the Church':

> The whole of existence is a mystery. The cosmos is a mystery; the world around us is a mystery; my own person is a mystery and my fellow human beings are a mystery. Although I understand much of these realities, none of them is capable of an exhaustive understanding on my part...
> [The Son of God] became the centre of the mystery of the most perfect active presence of the divine Transcendence within the creation, the centre of the creation raised to the highest and fullest union with God, raised to the status of supreme mystery *qua* church...[10]

Catholics in the West too, especially in France, have written books with the title *The Mystery of the Church* or some such. We think particularly of Yves Congar, who has dealt more adequately than most with this notion, though his book entitled in English *The Mystery of the Church*, a translation of two works, *Esquisses du Mystère de L'Eglise* and *La Pentecôte: Chartres* 1956,[11] does not actually contain a chapter on the Church as mystery. H. Clerissac is also author of a work entitled in English *The Mystery of the Church.*[12] This deals with the Church only as one of the mysteries of religion.

An exception to this pattern is R. F. Trevett's *L'Eglise et Son Mystère*, appearing in English as *The Church: Christ's Mystery and Sacrament.* This work not only roots the notion of mystery in Pauline usage but warns against watering it down to the jejune sense documented so far. Trevett writes:

> What then is the mystery of the Church? The word must be understood in the original sense of *Mysterion* as explained on several occasions by St Paul (*1 Cor* 2:7–8; *Rom* 16:25–27; *Col* 1:24–28; 2:2–4; *Eph* 3:3–12). Hence 'mystery' must not be watered down until it becomes only a hidden truth which the mind finds obscure. Mystery is an event produced by God's power and revealed by God in the very act of bringing it about. This event affects men and calls upon them to act. In fact, mystery is 'Christ among you' (*Col* 1:24–28), an infinite event of which the Church is one facet.

> In this sense and for this reason, the mystery of the Church consists in the interdependence, within her walls, of history and the eternity of God, of man and of God, of the visible and invisible. To use a more direct expression: the Church is the assembly of those who are baptised and inspired by supernatural faith in Jesus Christ. They recognise the authority of Peter, of the Apostles and their successors. And, *at the same time*, the Church is the instrument by means of which God in his mercy provides for the salvation of the whole human race. The mystery is the union of these two points of view. On the one hand, it is a human society, and on the other, it prolongs the existence of Christ.[13]

Equally satisfying because equally Pauline is John Powell's *The Mystery of the Church*, written in the wake of Vatican II. 'This plan of God to share his life and love with us, through the formation of a community established by his Son, Paul calls "the mystery hidden for ages and generations" (*Col* 1:26).'[14]

True sense of mystery

So what was the true meaning intended by Vatican II in presenting the Church as mystery? It was a meaning which the 1985 Synod perhaps inadequately reproduced while still singling this term out as basic to Vatican II ecclesiology. After a long period of debate in the Council sessions as to where emphasis should fall in this fundamental document on the Church in our time, the 1964 Constitution *Lumen Gentium* began not with hierarchy or laity but with a chapter on 'The mystery of the Church'. This was followed by a chapter on the biblical figure favoured for representing the larger notion, 'The People of God'. Although that biblical figure stole the limelight and received much theological attention in subsequent years, it is secondary to the initial idea of the Church as mystery. The Synod, for its own reasons, felt the need to reverse that trend.

Lumen Gentium presents the Church as mystery in a way that is generally faithful to the development of the notion in the Pauline literature of the New Testament. The mystery, which is not simply a matter beyond our understanding but a vast sacred reality that has in fact been revealed to us, is the mystery of Christ, the plan for all things that God designed for eternity to take effect 'in Christ' (in Paul's frequent phrase). So the Constitution speaks at once of Christ; the Church is the mystery of Christ in its ecclesial, community dimension. The mystery, the plan, also has historical and biblical dimensions, as does the Church. The text, therefore, proceeds to unfold the stages of historical development of the mystery that the Bible records and that the eternal Father planned in his wisdom—wisdom being another term which is basic to Pauline thinking and which evokes that particular concept of salvation history found in the Wisdom literature of the Old Testament (as distinct from patriarchal and prophetic versions). It is also a term beloved of the New Testament in general and Paul in particular. Those stages of development of the plan are also the phases of growth of the Church, as they are of the world itself. The Constitution reminds us of this by beginning with creation, again in fidelity to Paul and to Wisdom.[15] The plan as far as the Church is concerned (if not the world, for the moment) is for a participation/fellowship/share by human beings in divine life—*koinonia* in the language of the New Testament: the mystery of Christ is a mystery of life (another notion of Church the Synod will see as basic). In a significant series of participles the origin and growth of the Church are swiftly sketched, beginning with creation of the world and proceeding to the eschaton: 'foreshadowed... prepared for... established... made manifest... fulfilled.'[16] The mystery of Christ, which under this community aspect is the Church, has its origins in God's eternal decision, its development in salvation history, and its eventual fulfilment.

In two paragraphs of the Constitution we have learnt much about the Church as mystery. It is part of a divine eternal plan that is Christ. Paul spent his missionary and literary life endeavouring to plumb the latent significance of this. The Church shares this plan with the world. The community of people caught up in this mystery, this vast design, shares in life, just as the world itself receives existence as gift, life and existence both being bestowed by the divine benefactor. It is a plan worked out in history from the beginning, described in Old and New Testaments of the Bible, to the benefit of 'all good people from the time of Adam'.

In the paragraphs that follow, the trinitarian character of the mystery is outlined and the life and work of Jesus brought into focus. Two features are stressed: what Jesus came to do is expressed by the Synoptic Gospels as inauguration of God's *basileia* ('kingdom' is usually an unhappy translation). This work reaches its climax in Jesus' death and glorification, his Paschal Mystery (no simple 'puzzle' intended, but a sacred reality again, like other mysteries of his life, as the Rosary reminds us). The Constitution does not identify Church with *basileia*: the mystery of the Church is said to be manifest in Jesus' preaching of the *basileia*, and in her growth she strives to achieve its consummation.[17] Because the evangelists use this term to approximate to Paul's idea in *mysterion*, we shall look more closely at the idea of Church and *basileia* in chapters 3 and 4 below.

This first chapter of the Vatican II Constitution on the mystery of the Church also contains a section (6) on biblical images of Church.[18] Commentators, like the Abbot translator and Dulles, hasten to explain that the Church as mystery defies adequate understanding and so concrete figures are required. It would be better again to follow Paul in seeing this vast mystery as many-faceted (*polypoikilos* is his term at *Eph* 3:9: 'manifold' in the Revised Standard Version, 'many-coloured' in William Barclay's more literal version[19]—like Joseph's coat in *Genesis* 37). Seeing the mystery as many-faceted requires a range of images on the part of the biblical authors, who think graphically rather than attempt exhaustive definition. They have recourse to figures drawn from married love, family life, architecture, pastoral and agricultural labour. Each figure contributes something to our understanding of the totality of God's design for all his creation—the mystery of Christ—and in particular its community dimension, the Church.

Having thus with its opening chapter on mystery set the widest possible parameters for its consideration of Church, so escaping previous more limited expositions, the Council Fathers can then indulge a preference for one biblical figure, the People of God (which the 1985 Synod will later ignore), and set in place particular features of Church life, like hierarchic organisation and religious charism.

The contemporary Church, then, is content to describe itself as mystery, whatever the range of inspired images and figures available for partial illustration and whatever the appropriateness of one model or another thrown up by historical emphasis or theological elaboration of the day. The acceptance of mystery in ecclesiology is not a passing fad; it is an ineluctable decision, arrived at only in the wake of developments in study of the Fathers and the Scriptures, particularly the Pauline letters, where the term abounds. We are suggesting that it will no longer be found completely adequate to speak of Church in any other way, whichever facet of this many-faceted (*polypoikilos*) mystery one chooses to highlight for the moment in response to changing needs and conditions. This is not to suggest that any one term can do justice to the great reality, but rather to admit the relative adequacy of this concept of God's plan in its entirety. The Synod, for instance, we shall see selecting also communion, *koinonia*, for special contemporary emphasis, thanks to eloquent recommendation by certain hierarchies, notably that of England and Wales. The 1987 Synod on the laity would confirm this emphasis.[20] But, as we mentioned in pointing to New Testament thinking, this share in divine life that occurs within the Church is one feature of the divine plan for its human beneficiaries that is the mystery of Christ.

Biblical roots of mystery

In speaking of God's plan generally and the Church in particular as *mysterion*, Paul is employing a term that has its roots, not in Greek religion, where it is rather the plural that occurs, but in the Greek rendering of the Old Testament, particularly of an Aramaic term occurring in the book of *Daniel*. The background to the word has been studied thoroughly by Raymond Brown,[21] Gunther Bornkamm[22] and Chrys Caragounis. Caragounis's summary of the Old Testament sense of mystery is that it 'is God's purpose, it is eschatological, it has cosmic dimensions, and it is a unified plan'.[23] This is precisely the sense that is adopted in the Pauline letters of the New Testament, both those more directly associated with Paul's personal literary activity (proto-Pauline, to use a term devised to deal with the spectrum of involvement that is authorship in the ancient world) and those thought to be less directly associated (deutero-Pauline, including especially *Ephesians* and *Colossians*). As mentioned above, the term occurs only once in the Gospels, in that intriguing verse *Mk* 4:11, where *mysterion* is linked with *basileia*, the implications of which we shall have to examine later.

Before looking at some illuminating occurrences of 'mystery' in Paul for our study of Church, it is well to remark, as *Lumen Gentium* does, that he frequently associates it with 'wisdom', to the extent that the two words (and others, like 'purpose' and 'will') can for him be interchangeable for that sense of the vast sacred reality that is God's plan for all creation. Behind this usage, we have suggested, lies the highly significant and quite distinctive theology of the Wisdom literature of the Old Testament. In books like *Job, Wisdom, Sirach (Ecclesiasticus), Ecclesiastes, Baruch* it is the provident Lord of history who dominates the scene, not the God of the patriarchs of Torah and Prophets. This Lord is concerned not simply with one racial group but with all humanity, and beyond them with the whole cosmos. The world and its human community he conducts in his providence to fulfilment at the goal of salvation/liberation history.

Paul resonated strongly with this theology, this world view which has been neglected even today by biblical scholars electing for 'a canon within the canon'. He was concerned for the salvation of Jews and Gentiles both and impatient therefore with a parochial viewpoint, sensing as well the groaning of all creation for fulfilment.[24] In a range of letters he spoke of his mission to the Church and, more briefly, of the destiny of the world within the context of that immense design, conceived in the mind of God from eternity, implemented at 'the end of the times' 'in Christ' particularly through the Paschal Mystery of Jesus, and thus revealed more clearly in the post-resurrection era. He warmed to the hypostatisation of wisdom in those OT books, and presented Jesus (or Christ) as that figure in his letters. Of the seventeen occurrences of the term 'mystery' in the letters,[25] it is perhaps those in *Ephesians* that illustrate his thinking behind the mystery of Christ most amply:

> When you read this you can perceive my insight into the mystery of Christ, which was not made known to the sons of men in other generations as it has now been revealed to his holy apostles and prophets by the Spirit; that is, how the Gentiles are fellow heirs, members of the same body, and partakers of the promise in Christ Jesus through the gospel. Of this gospel I was made a minister according to the gift of God's grace which was given to me by the working of his power. To me, though I am the very least of all the saints, this grace was given, to preach to the Gentiles the unsearchable riches of Christ and to make all men see what is the plan of the mystery hidden for ages in God who created all things; that through the church the manifold wisdom of God might now be made known to the principalities and powers in the heavenly places. This was according to the eternal purpose which he has realised in Christ Jesus our Lord (*Eph* 3:4–11).

It is an eternal plan/purpose/mystery/wisdom only now becoming clear; it is a rich, multifaceted design affecting all things, though for Paul it is the share by the Gentiles in its community dimension that is most urgent. This mystery of Christ has taken effect through the life and death of Jesus (Paul's distinction in usage of the proper names is significant, if not consistent throughout all the letters: for him Christ *is* the mystery, the plan, 'the wisdom and...').

This is Paul's usage and thinking that lies behind later ecclesiastical usage, that disappears for a period, and surfaces again in recent times with the renaissance of patristic and biblical studies. To give the complete picture of the Pauline background there is need to mention that in some passages of the letters *mysterion* is employed to bring out not the full scope of the divine cosmic plan but some aspect of it. At 1 *Cor* 15:51 it is our resurrection that is in focus; at *Eph* 5:32 the New Testament's most profound theology of marriage is beautifully presented in a vision of this relationship encapsulating the whole mystery of Christ. By contrast 2 *Thess* 2:7 sees the obverse of the divine plan in 'the mystery of lawlessness', everything intended by the Father being frustrated through sin. Elsewhere in the New Testament beyond that single Gospel occurrence at *Mk* 4:11 the word is found only in three 'Pauline' occurrences in *Revelations*.

The Fathers and later theology

In choosing to present the Church basically and most adequately as mystery, Vatican II was thus returning to Paul and to terminology reaching back to Old Testament usage. It was also returning to a theology preserved as well in the writings of the patristic period following the composition of the New Testament. The apocalyptic document *The Shepherd of Hermas*, possibly as early as Pope Clement at the end of the first century, speaks of a vision of an elderly lady identified as the Church—elderly 'because she was created first of all; that is why she is elderly, and for her the world was made'.[26] The great catechist-theologian of Alexandria in the early third century, Origen, acknowledges Paul's thinking in sketching the beginnings of the Church:

> Do not think, I ask you, that his Bride, that is, the Church, is referred to only from the time of the

> Saviour's Incarnation, but from the beginning of the human race and even from the creation of the world—in fact, with Paul's encouragement I should look for the origin of this mystery more remotely, even before the creation of the world.[27]

Augustine, the giant of the West two centuries later, whom *Lumen Gentium* acknowledges in presenting the Church as mystery and outlining its development, concurs:

> The Church goes back a long way. From the time that saints have been so called, the Church has been on earth. At one time the Church was in Abel only... at one time in Enoch only... at one time in the house of Noah only... at one time in Abraham only.[28]

That Paul's terminology did not gain lasting favour was perhaps due to the use of 'mysteries' for the religious rites of pagan Greek religion. That his theology did not reach beyond the patristic period into medieval and modern times can be attributed to the decline in biblical and patristic studies that characterised those later ages and affected their theology. Ecclesiologists trace the move to institutional models following the Reformation by way of reaction against reformist theology. Even return to scriptural images of Church in this century did not encourage Catholic theologians generally to push on to the more adequate Pauline concept, so that its rediscovery by the Council (as opposed to Trent and Vatican I) came as a novelty, a novelty that has really not been appreciated for its antiquity and its adequacy. Even the 1985 Synod, we have seen, seems not to have fully understood it in pressing for its retention.

And yet, as always, there have been conspicuous exceptions to this short-sightedness, theologians able and willing to throw off the limitations of blinkered vision, risking thereby official displeasure for bypassing a theology of Church current even in magisterial statements of the day. In the years before Vatican II, the great French theologians Henri De Lubac and Yves Congar, teaching in their orders' theologates, ventured to go beyond the notion of Church as mystical Body of Christ—rich though it is as a biblical figure and yet less dynamic and less adequate—that gained currency and even obligation in the wake of the 1943 encyclical of Pope Pius XII. With their deep scholarship and wide acquaintance with the Fathers and the (whole) Bible, they were able as well as willing to see theological realities fully and not partially.

Just such a work of insight and scholarship arising out of familiarity with the sources was De Lubac's *The Splendour of the Church* published in the years between *Mystici Corporis Christi* and *Lumen Gentium.* His conviction is that, 'at a certain given state of crisis or point of maturation, one particular mystery—one particular part of the unique whole—comes, as it were, into the foreground of the reflexive landscape.'[29] Hence he opens with a chapter on 'The Church as mystery' in the belief that, 'as far as the development of doctrine is concerned, the twentieth century is destined to be "the century of the Church".'[30] For De Lubac, who can, like his race generally, be scholarly and expansive at once,

> the mystery of the Church is all mystery in little; it is our own mystery par excellence. It lays hold on the whole of us and surrounds us; for it is in his Church that God looks upon us and loves us, in her that he desires us and we encounter him, and in her that we cleave to him and are made blessed.[31]

Like Paul's many-faceted wisdom, the Church for De Lubac presents 'an infinite variety of harmonics'.[32] Like Paul he sees the mystery as vast in its extent: 'Following in the footsteps of St Thomas, we can give the name "Church" to that gigantic organism which includes all the host of the angels as well as men, and even extends to the whole cosmos as well,'[33] he says at the beginning of the chapter on 'The dimensions of the mystery'. As he traces the origins of the Church, his writing is a tissue of quotations from the biblical authors, the Fathers we quoted above, and St Thomas, all of whom he has at his fingertips:

> If we are to survey all its dimensions, in the focus of faith, we must go even deeper into the past. 'The ancient patriarchs already belonged to that same body of

> the Church which we constitute'; we have to look beyond Moses and the covenant of Sinai and beyond the promises made to 'our father Abraham' into the dawn of time. The Church, 'the sacrament of man's salvation,' is not the result of some fresh plan, as it were, on the part of God, nor of any 'belated pity'; it does not matter how far back you go, you still find her. Before the Law of Moses, the Church existed under the 'law of nature'; she exists 'ab exordio saeculi'. There has always been a people of God, and a vine which the Father tends unceasingly.[34]

For De Lubac the Church is the mystery of Christ—'so much so that the two names "Church" and "Christ" would seem to be interchangeable, as we can see as early as St Paul. That is where the expression "the mystical Christ" finds its basis, and St Augustine can say, in one of the nutshell paradoxes he loved so dearly: "Christ preaches through Christ".'[35] In the same sense he quotes his country's patron:

> Joan of Arc's words to her judges convey at one and the same time the depths of the mystique of belief and the practical good sense of the believer: 'It seems to me that it is all one, Christ and the Church, and that we ought not to make any difficulty of it.' These words of a simple believer are also a summing up of the faith of the Church's doctors.[36]

We would have to admit that, for all its novelty in magisterial statement, *Lumen Gentium's* presentation of the Church as mystery is hardly an advance on this chidden seminary professor's and that his later recognition was not premature. But magisterial incorporation of luminous theological elaboration does not always occur, and we are grateful to the Fathers of Vatican II for their theology of Church, even if, as we have seen, it was not fully understood.

If we are not as grateful to the 1985 Synod Fathers for their accent on mystery, it is because their accent falls a little awry and because theirs could be other than the serene, disinterested presentation of apostle, Fathers, theologian and Council. We have seen the Synod in their

Message to the People of God speaking of the 'spiritual note of mystery' which 'has as its first characteristic element the universal call to holiness'.[37] In similar vein, treatment of 'The mystery of the Church' in the Synod's *Final Report* begins against a backdrop of warnings of the spread of secularism and immanentism.[38] This negative tone responded well to the German bishops' expression of anxiety on the subject and to the view that the Council's Constitution on the Church in the Modern World, *Gaudium et Spes*,[39] had presented an unduly roseate picture of that world.[40] Another thrust of the German bishops' synodal interventions was to the effect that the postconciliar period had been marked excessively by debate over structure, so that, in the words of Cardinal Ratzinger, 'the Church has been reduced to its institutional aspect. It is essential, therefore, to put forward the Church as *mysterium*, transcending itself towards Christ'.[41]

That puts a different complexion on the accent on mystery to be found in the Synod's *Final Report*. One is inclined to see a motivation other than mere 'return to the sources' in that stress on holiness and interiority:

> The whole importance of the Church derives from her connection with Christ. The Council has described the Church in diverse ways: as the people of God, the body of Christ, the bride of Christ, the temple of the Holy Spirit, and family of God. These descriptions of the Church complete one another and must be understood in the light of the Mystery of Christ or of the Church in Christ. We cannot replace a false unilateral vision of the Church as merely hierarchical with a new sociological conception which is also unilateral. Jesus Christ is ever present in his Church and lives in her as risen. From the Church's connection with Christ we clearly understand the eschatological character of the Church herself (cf. *LG* 7). In this way the Church in its earthly wandering is the messianic people (cf. *LG* 9) that already anticipates in itself its future reality as a new creation. Yet she remains the Church that embraces sinners, that is holy yet ever needing purification and that presses onwards, amidst the per-

> secutions of this world and the consolations of God, towards the kingdom of the future.[42] In this sense there are always present within the Church the mystery of the Cross and the mystery of the resurrection.[43]

The Synod Fathers have accepted Wordsworth's sentiments that 'the world is too much with us,' that it is time to promote transcendence over immanence, spiritual reality over institution, and have decided (inaccurately) that 'mystery' represents that reversal of direction—hence the caption of *Die Zeit*, 'Flight into mystery'. Paul would not see the divine plan as involving any kind of retreat from the world, though he would appreciate emphasis on the Paschal Mystery of Jesus' Cross and Resurrection, the focal point of the mystery of Christ (even if its inclusion in that passage from the *Final Report* is more remedial than dogmatic in purpose).

T. S. Eliot's Thomas A'Becket in, ironically, *Murder in the Cathedral* rejects the temptation to martyrdom thus:

> The last temptation is the greatest treason:
> To do the right deed for the wrong reason.

It will be a pity if a Synod committed to promoting 'a better and complete investigation of the Second Vatican Council'[44] has the effect of obscuring the conciliar presentation of the Church by distorting the true sense of mystery developed so lucidly over the ages by theologians of the calibre of Paul, Origen and De Lubac. Thankfully, the following Synod, held in 1987 and devoted to the place of the laity in the Church and in the world, embraced the notion of Church as mystery wholeheartedly and unambiguously. This conviction emerges consistently from Pope John Paul II's post-synodal apostolic exhortation, *Christifideles Laici*,[45] of which Paul would not have been ashamed.

Mystery and sacrament

What perhaps encouraged the 1985 Synod Fathers to see in 'mystery' a solution to some of their concerns about the contemporary Church was the use of this word in early Christian history and recent European theology in association with 'sacrament', the latter Latin term being employed synonymously with Paul's Greek word. *Lumen Gentium*, in fact, at the opening of its treatment of the mystery of the Church makes the interchange: 'In Christ the Church is a kind of sacrament, or sign and instrument, of the intimate union of the whole human race with God.'[46] Only then does the Council document proceed to unfold the historical and biblical dimensions of the mystery of Christ which the Church also is, in the Pauline understanding of mystery.

The relationship of the two terms goes back to the earliest translations made of the Greek Scriptures for the benefit of Latin-speaking Christians. *Mysterion*, we have seen, occurs only once in the Gospels, at *Mk* 4:11 in Jesus' words about the share in the mystery of the kingdom given to the disciples; there, though most of these Old Latin translators simply transliterate the term (Jerome later in producing his authoritative, Vulgate, collation of these translations accepts the *mysterium* of the European translators), two translators in the then vigorous African Church show more initiative in opting for *sacramentum*, a word then used of keeping holy a contract or relationship, like a law or military oath. Augustine, bishop in Africa and often at odds with Jerome in things biblical, liked the new application of the term and developed it in the direction of later sacramental theology. 'Signs, when applied to divine things, are called *sacramenta*,'[47] he would say. 'In no type of religion, true or false, can people be associated unless linked together by some community of visible signs or *sacramenta*.'[48]

Though the twentieth century Council's phrasing is not markedly different from the fifth century bishop's, the description of the Church as sacrament in fact lapsed after patristic times until revived in German theology in the nineteenth century. In this century it was again the great French biblical-patristic-liturgical theologians, Congar and De Lubac, who gave the notion currency. De Lubac, whom we have seen as a splendid example of one who kept in touch with all those traditions and hence a 'traditional' theologian in the most dynamic sense, quotes the Roman liturgy in saying, 'We can say of the Church, as of Christ, "a great mystery and wonderful sacrament".'[49] Congar, in a chapter in his *Cette Eglise que J'Aime* entitled 'Universal sacrament of salvation', speaks, like the Council, of the Church as sacrament because it is both sign and instrument together:

> The sacraments, and the Church herself as great sacrament, are the place where the *past*, which is Christ as covenant and saviour, is *present* in view of the *future* of the world, by the operation of the Holy Spirit. There is sacrament, where the world to come, *vita venturi saeculi*, having come to us in Jesus Christ, touches the present world to draw it towards eschatological fulfilment.[50]

Congar parallels the words mystery and mystical with sacrament and sacramental at that point as he does later in discussing the term 'sacrament of the neighbour'. He accepts the term and improves on it by referring to the neighbour as a mystery 'in the precise and traditional sense of the word'. But he reminds us of the difference between that usage and the use of 'sacrament' of the Church: 'The Church is the universal sacrament of salvation instituted for everyone and sufficient for everyone, the only one therefore truly suited to gather all people together in one unique and visible People of God, Body of Christ and Temple of the Holy Spirit.'[51]

The writings of these men in the first half of this century popularised the notion of Church as sacrament. At the Second Vatican Council the German bishops in particular are credited with influencing the Constitution on the Church in this direction, and we can now recognise this aspect of mystery in places in *Lumen Gentium* where Augustinian echoes are audible:

> Christ, sole mediator, established his holy Church, community of faith, hope and charity, here on earth as a visible structure and ceaselessly sustains it as the means of communicating truth and grace to everyone.

> The society equipped with hierarchical forms and the Mystical Body of Christ are not, however, to be regarded as two separate realities, nor the visible assembly and the spiritual community, nor the earthly Church and the Church endowed with heavenly goods; instead, they form one interwoven reality comprising a human and a divine element. Hence the Church is compared with the mystery of the Incarnate Word by a quite remarkable analogy: just as the nature he assumed served the Divine Word as a living instrument of salvation indissolubly united to him, in a similar way the communal structure of the Church serves the Spirit of Christ, who gives it life, for the growth of the body.[52]

Not that the Catholic community alone has reached this understanding of Church. The World Council of Churches since 1927 has been discussing the sacramental nature of the Church; and the meeting of its Faith and Order Commission in Louvain in 1971 spoke of the Church as:

> the sign by which God's all-embracing love is visible in this world. It is not only a symbolic image. It is a sign, because the living Christ wishes to be, and is, present in our midst. It *is* a sign. But it is also no more than a sign. The mystery of the love of God is not exhausted through this sign, but, at best, just hinted from afar. So just as the church can be understood in this way as a sacrament or sign, its oneness can also be understood as a sign.[53]

The attempt to relate sacrament to mystery is most interesting here. Likewise, for the Orthodox community the sacramental nature of the Church is traditional teaching: 'It is the common foundation of the ecclesiologies of East and West,' wrote Congar in hope in 1982.[54]

Conclusion

The profundity of an ecclesiology founded on an understanding of the biblical import of mystery and its patristic development makes more regrettable the relative abundance of theological writing displaying an impoverished appreciation of the notion and the scarcity of writers in touch with its biblical and patristic roots. Thankfully, a Church Council of this century was able to capitalise on the scholarship and insights of just such perceptive theologians and incorporate them in a statement, itself now in danger of being ignored or misunderstood. Misrepresentation of mystery in ecclesiology may, we have seen, be made in the hope of dealing with some present concern about the contemporary Church, such as its need for greater interiority. But the price paid for this distortion, apart from the encouragement for some theologians to see mystery as a neoconservative tendency in ecclesiology akin to a descending Christology,[55] is to sacrifice the immense advantage of a permanently adequate ecclesiology to the Catholic community. If we adhere to Pauline understanding of Church as mystery, we have the possibility of response to continuing questions about the origin of the Church, about membership of the Church, about its relation to Christ, its relevance to the wider world, its ultimate destiny, and the various dimensions of this many-faceted mystery. Apostle and Fathers appreciated this in their time, and we should prize it in ours.

Points for discussion

1. In your experience, are Christian people these days preoccupied with the meaning of Church, in the way De Lubac forecast would happen this century? In what ways does such an interest manifest itself? Do people succeed in seeing Church as mystery? If not, how do they see Church and their place in it?
2. One advantage of meditating on the mystery of the Church is that we can better evaluate her institutional character. How far are Catholics in particular locked into this aspect of Church—authority, power, laws, submission, office-bearers, organisation, finance? To what extent is an institutional character appropriate to Christian thinking on Church? Does the notion of Church as sacrament help?
3. Do you think an understanding of Church as mystery

will help communion between Christian churches? How will it affect current divisions? Can this notion of mystery extend even to an appreciation of all world religions?

4. Ministry follows membership in the Church. It has been understood too exclusively, as though confined to the ordained; it can, on the other hand, be applied indiscriminately. Does a vision of Church as mystery help us avoid these extremes?
5. Do you find any comfort in those words of St Joan of Arc (p.14 above), 'It seems to me that it is all one, Christ and the Church, and that we ought not to make any difficulty of it'?

2

A MYSTERY OF LIFE

In 1964, during the Second Vatican Council and before the appearance of its Constitution on the Church, there appeared in English a work written two years earlier by the French Dominican, Jerome Hamer, entitled *The Church is a Communion.*[1] The title had a strange ring about it to English-speaking Catholics: 'Church' they were familiar with, 'Communion' usually referred to Holy Communion, the sacrament of the Blessed Eucharist, so that Hamer's point, clearer perhaps to French readers in the original title *L'Eglise est une Communion*, was not immediately obvious. Hamer's French word, of course, and its transliteration was meant to denote sharing, fellowship, participation—the sense of the New Testament term *koinonia*, which comes from the adjective *koinos*, 'common' and means making common to others what is personal to oneself. The fact that this meaning did not immediately emerge from 'Communion' is probably a reflection on Catholics' understanding then, and perhaps today, of the Eucharist.

Twenty-five years later we respond better to Hamer's intention in that title, thanks especially to the insistence of the 1985 Extraordinary Synod of Bishops and their *Final Report*, itself responding to synodal speakers, notably Cardinal Danneels and, on behalf of the hierarchy of England and Wales, Cardinal Hume.[2] Though the *Final Report* insists that 'the ecclesiology of communion is the central and fundamental idea of the Council's documents... And so much was done by the Second Vatican Council so that the Church as communion might be more clearly understood and concretely incorporated into life'[3], even readers of that Council's documents (not by far the majority of Catholics, as the Synod admitted) would be unaware of this ecclesiology infusing its pages.

In the previous chapter we have, in fact, highlighted the Council's initial emphasis on the church as mystery and commented on the adequacy and appropriateness of this notion, from a biblical and patristic viewpoint in particular. We also admitted the degree of attention that fell rather on the biblical figure for this notion, the People of God, at the time of promulgation of the Council's Constitution on the Church. The Synod we saw downplaying the latter and re-interpreting the former. Neither Dominican theologian nor Council document really succeeded in bringing to the fore the notion of Church as communion/fellowship/sharing/participation—*koinonia*, in short.

A mystery of life

And yet, as we hinted above on p.7, a conspicuous feature and function of the mystery of Christ, this divine plan, is the communication of LIFE. John's Jesus comes within that plan 'that they may have life' (10:10), and he defines himself pre-eminently in the words 'I am the LIFE' (14:6), and insofar as he is Life in person he is also the Way and the Truth. In *koinonia* he comes to share with us, make common (*koinos*), what God has as his own: life, not just existence, though there is that as well, but 'life to the full'. The First Letter of John says it all, personally but most theologically (1 *Jn* 1:1–4). The writer says he is about to tell them of life, but not just life in the abstract: he has met Life in person, shaken him by the hand, because God has shared that life with him in Jesus. And that sharing/fellowship/communion/*koinonia* is to be extended with the Johannine community by the letter, and other ways:

> Our theme is the Word which is life. We tell you of what was there from the beginning, of what we heard, and saw with our own eyes, of what we looked at, and touched with our own hands. This life is full displayed for all to see. We saw it, and we speak from personal experience. It is news of this eternal life, which was with the Father, and which was fully displayed to us,

> that we are now bringing to you. We bring you the message of what we saw and heard. We do so because we have fellowship (*koinonia*) with God and with his Son Jesus Christ, and we want you to share with us in that fellowship. We are writing this to you, because we want our joy to be complete.[4]

Though most of the 18 occurrences of *koinonia* in the New Testament (it is hardly found at all in the OT) are in Paul's letters, it is John at this place who provides us with a synthesis of this divine and human fellowship, combining its vertical and horizontal dimensions. The initiative lies with God; the means is the Incarnation. Through the Son in his incarnate life we enjoy a fellowship not only with him but with the Father, which is a thought nowhere else expressed; we receive a share in the eternal life that the Son also enjoys and so eminently displays in his incarnate existence. And it is possible for us, having ourselves received the gift of life by responding to the Word of life, to share it with others. It is not a private gift, as God himself did not allow it to remain; it is to be made common, *koinos*, in fellowship, communion, sharing, *koinonia*.

The nature of this shared gift is clarified further in Paul and the single occurrence of *koinonia* in *Acts*. It is a share with the Son (1 *Cor* 1:9) in the Spirit (2 *Cor* 13:13, *Phil* 2:1), a share in faith (*Phlm* 6) and in the Gospel (in the sense of a response to the Gospel: *Phil* 1:5). It is a share in the Eucharist, in the Body and Blood of Christ (1 *Cor* 10:16–17), and in his sufferings and glory (*Phil* 3:10–11).

Because of these aspects of *koinonia* and the very root of the word, the implications for ecclesiology are patent and ineluctable, and yet, as we have noted, the presentation of this aspect of the Church as mystery has until recently been muted in theological and magisterial statement. Only with the work of Catholic and Anglican contributors to the International Commission (ARCIC) and their final report in 1981 did unanimity emerge: 'In the early Christian traditions, reflection on the experience of *koinonia* opened the way to the understanding of the mystery of the Church.'[5] The English cardinal echoed this position in speaking to the 1985 Synod on:

> ...the concept of the Church as *communio* or *koinonia*. This word helps us to penetrate more deeply the mystery which the Church is. This concept means a gathering together of those who give themselves in faith to Jesus Christ and who receive the gift of the Holy Spirit when they are reborn by baptism in the risen Lord. In this mutual and vital exchange between God and man, the faithful recognise their unity of life in Christ and their need for each other.[6]

Why were the implications of *koinonia* for ecclesiology slow to be recognised? Largely because of the interpretation of influential German (Protestant) exegetes, notably H. Seesemann in the 1930s, who opposed taking *koinonia* in any ecclesial sense and with whose work Hamer had to come to grips in writing his book on the Church as communion, and E. Käsemann, who even as late as 1963 advised the World Council of Churches meeting in Montreal against finding any such common ecclesiology in Paul and John.[7] Since then, happily, the New Testament evidence for *koinonia* has been re-evaluated, including that occurrence at *Acts* 2:42 that speaks of the Christians in the wake of Pentecost devoting themselves to the apostles' teaching and to fellowship, to the breaking of the bread and the prayers. An Indian scholar coming to the material from a different cultural background, George Panikulam says of this reference: 'This *koinonia* is the effect of the working of the Spirit in the community. It is based on faith, finds its expression in cult and its concrete realisation in the sharing of material goods.'[8] For Panikulam the Pauline usage of *koinonia* is also always communitarian in reference:

> Paul never uses *koinonia* for the individual sharing of someone in Christ. It is always used for someone's sharing in Christ with others. This leads to the conclusion that *koinonia* in Paul has a strict communitarian sense. 'When Paul wished to indicate the inwardness of the fellowship for each individual Christian,' observes Jourdan, 'he did it by means of another phrase *en Christo einai* [to be in Christ].' The soteriology and ecclesiology of Paul thus could be brought to a

koinonia. Fellowship with Christ is for him salvation, and fellowship with one another in Christ is for him the ideal Christian community.[9]

To complete the New Testament evidence for a communion ecclesiology, the First Letter of John supplies the vertical dimension of *koinonia* and the accent on life.

The picture is complete; theology and (hierarchical) magisterium now find no problems in developing the implicit ecclesiology, as ARCIC and the 1985 Synod have done:

> *Koinonia*/communion, founded on the Sacred Scripture, have been held in great honour in the early Church and in the Oriental Churches to this day... What does the complex word 'communion' mean? Fundamentally it is a matter of communion with God through Jesus Christ, in the Holy Spirit. This communion is to be had in the Word of God and in the sacraments. Baptism is the door and the foundation of communion in the Church; the Eucharist is the source and the culmination of the whole Christian life. The communion of the Eucharistic Body of Christ signifies and produces, that is, builds up, the intimate communion of all the faithful in the Body of Christ which is the Church.[10]

Though the Synod at that point does not also include reference to sharing Jesus' Cross and Resurrection, its stress on that elsewhere, as we have mentioned, was such as to give rise to comment on a change of emphasis from Vatican II.[11] The 1987 Synod would deal with the laity in the Church without such change of emphasis.[12]

The ARCIC document consistently labours the same first principle:

> Union with God in Christ Jesus through the Spirit is the heart of Christian *koinonia.* Among the various ways in which the term *koinonia* is used in different New Testament contexts, we concentrate on that which signifies a relation between persons resulting from their participation in one and the same reality. The Son of God has taken to himself our human nature, and he has sent upon us his Spirit, who makes us so

> truly members of the body of Christ that we too are able to call God 'Abba, Father'. Moreover, sharing in the same Holy Spirit, whereby we become members of the same body of Christ and adopted children of the same Father, we are also bound to one another in a completely new relationship. *Koinonia* with one another is entailed by our *koinonia* with God in Christ. This is the mystery of the Church.[13]

The World Council of Churches in its constitution defines itself as 'a fellowship of churches which confess the Lord Jesus Christ as God and Saviour according to the scriptures and therefore seek to fulfil together their common calling to the glory of the one God, Father, Son and Holy Spirit.' In its 1982 Lima document[14] it deals with the sacraments of Baptism and Eucharist within the context of *koinonia*, as we shall see.

Orthodox theologians are naturally comfortable with such an ecclesiology, speaking particularly of 'participation' (of the whole universe, a pregnant thought we shall touch on later) in the Creator's perfections and emphasising characteristically the vertical dimension of *koinonia* and the role of the Spirit. The ecclesiology, expressed here by Dumitru Staniloae, thus begins with divine transcendence:

> God brought the created world into being as a form of existence (other than his own) only in order to permit it to be filled with his perfections... By his human nature, which he united with his person, the Son of God ceaselessly remains among us human beings as an active presence, and is thus able all the more easily to communicate his divine perfections to us. He thereby became the centre of the mystery of the most perfect active presence of the divine Transcendence within the creation, the centre of the creation raised to the highest and fullest union with God, raised to the status of supreme mystery *qua* church. All who enter into communication (communion) with Christ as divine-human Person become in an enlarged sense his body, or his members, drawing even the world of things into this relationship with him.[15]

Yves Congar, who has explored the possibilities of dialogue between the 'sister churches' further than anyone else in the Catholic community, works throughout his *Diversity and Communion* from a basis of *koinonia* and its implications for unity and diversity in the Christian Church.

Koinonia, a share in life with others

Despite the rarity of occurrence of *koinonia* in the (Greek) Old Testament, Christians' experience from the beginning has been of fellowship, communion. Our earliest creeds, outside the brief Christological expressions of the New Testament, include reference to the communion of saints, the fellowship of those in this world and the next who have responded as 'saints' to Christ's offer of life. Augustine saw it was therefore beyond dispute that this community knows no national or racial boundaries, being based on an all-pervasive sharing: 'No commentator is required for the testimonies of the canonical Scriptures highlighting the fact that the Church consists in fellowship of the whole world (*in totius orbis communione*).'[16]

Modern theologians likewise have seen that this is what Church is eminently about—a share in life. De Lubac, admitting her institutional character, says that 'even more than an institution, she is a life that is passed on...this mystery of unity and life'. She cuts across the diversities that confound our common human nature:

> Any historian who retains the distinctively human hunger for communion with his fellowmen cannot help feeling continually the pathos of this situation. Yet that pathos leaves the Church out of account. And there, startlingly, is the wonderful phenomenon: a sudden closeness of those very men who seemed to have least in common and to be doomed, on every account, to irremediable separation. There is a brotherhood of common responses; they answer the same appeal and enjoy the same communion in the same love; it is as if one and the same blood flowed in their veins. They are children of the same Church and have all had from her the inheritance of the same Christ;

fed by the same faith, they are 'given to drink by the same Spirit,' who produces in them one and the same spontaneous reaction, and thus provides the sign by which they recognise one another.[17]

Hamer, too, struggling two decades ago to withstand the philological arguments of Seesemann, knew intuitively and by experience that the Church is about this share in life:

> Seesemann goes beyond his premises when he concludes that *koinonia* can throw no light on the concept of the Church. This seems to me to lose sight of the fact that *koinonia* in the New Testament denotes *a way of living* (being and acting), a relation with God and with men characteristic of the Christian community. Thus, even though the word *koinonia* is not synonymous with Church in the sense of a social group, it nevertheless signifies the mutual relations of Christians among themselves in their common dependence on Christ and the Spirit. We are at the very heart of the mystery of the Church.[18]

So before we can properly appreciate the ecclesiastical institution and deal with its implications and problems, we need to see the underlying community sharing the divine gift of life. It is that realisation that makes the ARCIC statements so exemplary; in dealing with thorny issues of intercommunion such as authority, they begin where John began with the divided Johannine community:

> The confession of Christ as Lord is the heart of the Christian faith. To him God has given all authority in heaven and on earth. As Lord of the Church he bestows the Holy Spirit to create a communion of men with God and with one another. To bring this *koinonia* to perfection is God's eternal purpose. The Church exists to serve the fulfilment of this purpose when God will be all in all.[19]

Acceptance of this principle will not solve all the difficulties confronting Christian unity today any more than it did in the early Church. Dulles speaks critically of the obscurity a communion ecclesiology leaves regarding the relationship between the spiritual and visible dimensions of the

Church.[20] Historians point to the disputes over sacramental discipline in the first few centuries of the Church, with Cyprian in Africa in 256 claiming his right to an opinion 'without depriving others of their claim on fellowship (*communio*) for thinking differently'.[21] Augustine later commented approvingly on this attitude: 'He concedes that I have the right not only to continue to seek the truth but also to arrive at a different opinion, without forfeiting my claim on *communio*.'[22] Other serious disagreements between Christians have occurred over the centuries. We shall look later at the vast question of unity and diversity in the Church, so germane is it to the notion of *koinonia*. At this point it is enough to say that there comes a time when people prefer to return to the principle that lies at the root of their Christian existence together in Church, the principle of shared divine life, the better to deal with the more episodic problems arising at a different level, lest these problems obscure the fact of shared life.

There is no admission here that *koinonia* speaks only to the heart as an interior principle. John related it to the incarnate Word of Life he had seen, heard and touched; Luke saw it at work in a sharing community; Paul invoked its implications for his collection for the Jerusalem church (*Rom* 15:26; 2 *Cor* 8:4; 9:13). All three saw the Communion of Saints taking sacramental form—'a double mystery of communication and communion,' says De Lubac of the Church, 'since by the communication of the sacraments—holy things (*sancta*)—she is a communion of holy ones (*sancti*).'[23] A more recent commentator gives the sacramental character of *koinonia* an even deeper theological foundation: because there is a communion in the Holy Spirit, there must be a communion of the saints, which requires communion in sacraments.[24] We have seen Augustine arguing, if only from an anthropological standpoint, that a community of people need *sacramenta* for the permanence of their association. The ARCIC agreement concedes as much:

> The Church as *koinonia* requires visible expression because it is intended to be the 'sacrament' of God's

saving work. A sacrament is both sign and instrument. The *koinonia* is a sign that God's purpose in Christ is being realised in the world by grace. It is also an instrument for the accomplishment of this purpose, inasmuch as it proclaims the truth of the Gospel and witnesses to it by its life, thus entering more deeply into the mystery of the Kingdom. The community thus announces what it is called to become.[25]

For Paul the call to *koinonia* with the Son, arising from the Father's faithfulness (1 *Cor* 1:9), is sealed in baptism—*one* baptism, not the variety claimed by the Corinthian factions. From that baptism comes also a share in the Son's sufferings and consequently in his resurrection (*Phil* 3:10–11). Panikulam explains this: 'What the apostle expounds as his experience is the experience of every Christian starting with the baptism: living the life-long state of death to the flesh and the world, in the constant move towards the resurrection and final glorification... the vocation to the fellowship with the Son starts in baptism and grows through the daily Christian life to the accomplishment.'[26] The Lima document develops this theology of baptism with further New Testament support:

> Baptism means participating in the life, death and resurrection of Jesus Christ. Jesus went down into the river Jordan in solidarity with sinners in order to fulfil all righteousness (*Mt* 3:15). This baptism led Jesus along the way of the Suffering Servant, made manifest in his sufferings, death and resurrection (*Mk* 10:38–40,45). By baptism, Christians are immersed in the liberating death of Christ where their sins are buried, where the 'old Adam' is crucified with Christ, and where the power of sin is broken. Those thus baptised are no longer slaves to sin, but free. Fully identified with the death of Christ, they are buried with him and are raised here and now to a new life in the power of the resurrection of Jesus Christ, confident that they will also ultimately be one with him in a resurrection like his (*Rom* 6:3–11; *Col* 2:13; 3:1; *Eph* 2:5–6).[27]

The share in life with others that *koinonia* means and to which baptism introduces the Christian community is extended to a share in the body and blood of Christ (1 *Cor* 10:16–17): the baptised community becomes a Eucharistic community. St John Damascene in the eighth century pointed up the implications for fellowship that Paul intended: 'It is called *koinonia*, and it really is, for through it we have fellowship with Christ and partake of his flesh and divinity. But through it we also have *koinonia* among ourselves and are united with one another. Since we receive one bread, we all become one Body of Christ and one blood, and members of one another. We are united in one Body of Christ.'[28] There is no escaping the communitarian (and sacramental) sense of *koinonia* brought out by Paul and John Damascene in this context, and yet, as we saw, there are those for whom (holy) communion is a private thing, with little sense of community commitment. The Synod makes a quiet protest against this attitude; the Lima document is much more strident:

> All kinds of injustice, racism, separation and lack of freedom are radically challenged when we share in the body and blood of Christ. Through the eucharist the all-renewing grace of God penetrates and restores human personality and dignity. The eucharist involves the believer in the central event of the world's history. As participants in the eucharist, therefore, we prove inconsistent if we are not actively participating in this ongoing restoration of the world's situation and the human condition.[29]

Paul, of course, would agree that this is what communion, fellowship, *koinonia* involves, as did the Council of Jerusalem in approving his mission to the Gentiles on the sole condition that he 'remember the poor' (*Gal* 2:10). He had already done so by bringing proceeds of his collection, made on the basis of *koinonia*, to Jerusalem on that occasion, and he continued to insist that by *koinonia* membership in the community meant sensitivity to the needs of those rendered less well-off by famine or (as at Jerusalem) hostility. Luke's description of the community in *Acts* suggests the sensitivity continued. And from Justin's description of Sunday Mass in the second century, which corresponds closely to our own, it is clear the sense of the Eucharistic *koinonia* was retained:

> Those who are well-off and willing give freely whatever they choose; the collection is then deposited with the president, who supports orphans, widows, those who are in want owing to sickness or any other cause, those who are in prison and strangers who are on a journey, and in brief takes care of all who are in need.[30]

At another and more basic level of sacramentality, this community sharing divine life is a community of the Word. For John it was his personal encounter with the Word of Life that brought him into fellowship with the Father; and it is through the Word that he introduces his community into this fellowship. Their response to his good news is meant to be akin to that expected of the Philippians by Paul when, to his joy, he thanks God for their '*koinonia* in the Gospel from the very first day until now' (*Phil* 1:5), a response they will extend to the 'good work' of Christian life and evangelising. As ARCIC says:

> The *koinonia* is grounded in the word of God preached, believed and obeyed. Through this word the saving work of God is proclaimed. In the fulness of time this salvation was realised in the person of Jesus, the Word of God incarnate. Jesus prepared his followers to receive through the Holy Spirit the fruit of his death and resurrection, the culmination of his life of obedience, and to become the heralds of salvation. In the New Testament it is clear that the community is established by a baptism inseparable from faith and conversion, that its mission is to proclaim the Gospel of God, and that its common life is sustained by the eucharist. This remains the pattern for the Christian Church.[31]

The community's response to the Word, of course, is a response of faith and love. The Philippians have brought joy to Paul by so responding, and he prays (1:10) that their love 'may abound more and more'. Writing to Philemon to make a request in fellowship, he begins by acknowledging the faith and love of his friend for Jesus and the community; and he expresses the hope that this '*koinonia* in faith' (*Phlm* 6) will translate itself into a loving act of forgiveness and an acceptance of the truth that all members of the community, slave and free, are equal. For his own troubled community, of course, John saw that to fail to love was to be false to the divine initiative of life and destructive of fellowship:

> Beloved, let us love one another; for love is of God, and he who loves is born of God and knows God. He who does not love does not know God; for God is love. In this the love of God was made manifest among us, that God sent his only Son into the world, so that we might live through him. In this is love, not that we loved God but that he loved us and sent his Son to be the expiation for our sins. Beloved, if God so loved us, we also ought to love one another. No man has ever seen God; if we love one another, God abides in us and his love is perfected in us (1 *Jn* 4:7–12).

Community and communities

We have seen Augustine insisting on his beautiful, irresistible ecclesiology, 'the Church consists of fellowship (*communio*) of the whole world'. And we have spent some time elaborating, with the particular help of Paul and John, on some of the many aspects of this vision of Church as *koinonia*, a share in life occurring within the divine plan that is the mystery of Christ. It is Augustine also who points out the obverse of this truth in his further claim: 'I am in the Church, whose members are those churches that we know from the canonical Letters to have been born as well as consolidated by the labours of the Apostles; fellowship (*communio*) with them I shall never forsake—so help me God—be it in Africa or wherever.'[32]

There is a beautiful balance here between Church universal and local, the one and the many, unity and pluriformity—all enjoying *koinonia*. A communion ecclesiology is clearly better adapted to accommodate the Augustinian truths than are many others. Hence Christian groups today can generally be found to be speaking in these terms and invoking such an ecclesiology, the World Council of Churches being one, as we observed from their constitution above, Vatican II being another, unlike its predecessors these last few hundred years. *Lumen Gentium*, after concentrating on the universal Church, proceeds to deal with individual bishops in particular churches, quoting Cyprian on 'the one Church divided throughout the whole world into many members'.[33] In this it was echoed by the 1985 Synod. ARCIC, perhaps out of regard for reformed tendencies generally, begins with the communities:

> The *koinonia* is realised not only in the local Christian communities, but also in the communion of these communities with one another. The unity of local communities under one bishop constitutes what is commonly meant in our two communions by 'a local church', though the expression is sometimes used in other ways. Each local church is rooted in the witness of the apostles and entrusted with the apostolic mission. Faithful to the Gospel, celebrating the one eucharist and dedicated to the service of the same Lord, it is the Church of Christ. In spite of diversities each local church recognises its own essential features in the others and its true identity with them.[34]

At least from the time of Pope Paul VI Rome has been using the term 'sister churches' in addressing the heads of the Eastern churches, who like Patriarch Athenagoras have replied in kind. In 1967 one such communication from the Pope read:

> In each local church the mystery of divine love is at work. Is this not the reason for that fine traditional expression, 'sister churches', which local churches love to use of one another? We have lived this life of sister churches for centuries, celebrating together the ecumenical councils which defended the deposit of faith against any alteration. Now after a long period of division and mutual incomprehension, the Lord has allowed us to rediscover ourselves as sister churches, despite the obstacles with which we had been con-

fronted. In the light of Christ, we see how urgent is the need to transcend these obstacles, so that we can bring to its fulness and perfection the communion existing between us, which is already so rich.[35]

'The communion existing between us' has proved to be fundamental to the ecumenical movement, as Cardinal Hume acknowledged at the 1985 Synod:

> The concept of Church as *communio* has been crucial to the dialogue conducted within the Anglican Roman Catholic International Commission. We have come to understand how together we are a part of a real but not yet complete *koinonia* or *communio*. This concept provides a context, too, in which the respective roles of Peter and the bishops can be understood and accepted without compromising the clear teaching of the first Vatican Council.[36]

There is among the Christian churches, and always has been, a real communion. That it is not yet (and never was?) complete we know from personal experience and our knowledge of history. Both these truths need emphasising together—in an eschatological perspective that keeps us looking ahead to the 'fulness and perfection' of which Paul VI spoke to Athenagoras. We can easily document the fact of diversity as we have the *koinonia* of New Testament and modern times. The New Testament does reflect churches organised on different lines, as Käsemann and others have reminded us. Some centuries later Augustine found this to be true, acknowledged it as inevitable, while placing limits to the degree of diversity:

> There are things which vary according to places and regions... There is freedom of observance in connection with all these kinds of things. There is no better practice for a wise and prudent Christian than to conform to the usages of the church in which he is. For anything that is neither against the faith nor against good morals must be treated as a matter of indifference and observed with due regard for those in whose society one lives.[37]

This is the thesis of Yves Congar, whose *Diversity and Communion* surveys the unity and pluriformity of Christian churches from the beginning, especially the relations of East and West. He finds axiomatic, among a fine collection of patristic data, the advice of St Irenaeus tendered to Pope Victor about the year 190 to dissuade him from excommunicating the Quartodeciman Christians of Asia (so called for celebrating Easter on 14 Nisan and breaking their fast that day):

> Such a diversity of observances has not just arisen now, in our time, but dates from long ago, from our forebears... They all nevertheless keep the peace, as do we, one with another: *the difference in the fast confirms the agreement in the faith.*[38]

Eusebius records the incident in his Church history, as he does the identical disagreement between Polycarp of Smyrna and Pope Anicetus, who nevertheless agreed to 'share communion with one another': excommunication, rupturing that communion (Irenaeus's 'peace' signified the same fellowship), was not condign in the circumstances of liturgical diversity alone which, in Irenaeus's words, merely accentuated the unity of faith. Congar proceeds to cite the difficult process in the early Church of distilling an 'orthodoxy'. 'The history of christological and trinitarian dogma is an illustration of this. One has only to think of the difficulties encountered over the terms *hypostasis*, *physis* and *ousia*. That did not prevent people from living, as a church, by *the reality* of Christ and his spirit, any more than it did in the apostolic age: they lived by faith and by the continuity of the apostolic confession of this faith.'[39] More recent shibboleths come to mind: should they be the occasion for rupturing communion? It is interesting to see the Synod briefly distinguishing pluralism from legitimate pluriformity.

Predictably, the churches are finding in *koinonia* not only an historical basis but an adequate ecclesiological principle for dealing with unity and diversity in Church life today. John and Paul had only to remind the churches of their day of the origin and responsibilities of the life they shared, though they too drew limits to communion on the part of those who could not respond in faith to the Word of

Life. In the Church, in the mystery of Christ, life 'to the full' is on offer: that is the purpose of a mystery in which 'the God and Father of our Lord Jesus Christ... has blessed us with every spiritual blessing, because our life is bound up with the life of Christ' (*Eph* 1:3).[40]

A share in existence with other creatures

The beauty of a biblically rooted theology of Church as mystery and *koinonia*, echoed also in patristic commentators, is its breadth of perspective, even if found by some to be short on institutional nicety. The Pauline mystery, because of the very terms of Paul's commission, is anything but parochial or discriminatory. Not only does it include all peoples, like Augustine's *communio*; it embraces as well all else created by God. Influenced to some extent by the Wisdom writing of earlier ages, Paul could see that the divine plan encompassed the whole of creation and would bring together 'all things, things in heaven and things on earth' (*Eph* 1:10). That is what the mystery of Christ in its completeness means. The Church, of course, represents particularly its community dimension for its human beneficiaries.

The sharing and participation that *koinonia* brings us with the Creator likewise extends beyond us to all existing things. Clement of Alexandria says beautifully, 'Just as the will of God is an act and is called the world, so also his intention is the salvation of people and is called the Church.'[41] Clearly, all that exists participates in that which God has by nature and has shared with all creation in *koinonia*. Eastern theologians, we have seen, like to meditate on this breadth of participation in the divine:

> The relationship of the world to its absolute Creator and Sustainer defines and augments its character as a mystery. In its existence the power of its Creator and Sustainer is manifested even though, on the one hand, he transcends it. The mystery of the world and the mystery of humanity are seen as an active presence of

> the absolutely Transcendent in their existence. But the world's own relationship with the Transcendent is itself a mystery... This bond between the world and its creator is 'participation' according to St Athanasius of Alexandria... God brought the created world into being as a form of existence (other than his own) only in order to permit it to be filled with his perfections.[42]

Paul would perhaps quarrel with Clement's suggestion that the divine intention envisages an eschaton only for human creation (cf. *Rom* 8:18–23). Theologians even as conservative as St Thomas would like to extend the Church to include the whole of creation. For the moment, however, we should raise briefly the participation that the world has in the divine gifts, and leave till later the question of the Church's relationship to it, recommending in passing that we retain the Bible's breadth of vision. To think of the Church in terms of *koinonia* both retains that vast perspective of the divine plan and focusses on the object of the plan, the mystery for us—a share in divine life. It is a share that comes from the Father, mediated through the Son, accepted in faith in the Word and reception of the Eucharist. It is a life enjoyed with others, a 'fellowship of the whole world', enlivening each community and allowing for a communion of communities. The Church is indeed a mystery of life.

Points for discussion

1. How familiar are you with the principal documents of the Second Vatican Council, especially its Constitution on the Church, *Lumen Gentium*? Read its #8 again, and also if possible the *Final Report* of the 1985 Synod of Bishops that looked back on Vatican II's teaching on the Church. Would you agree with the Synod that 'the central and fundamental idea' of that Council's teaching was of the Church as communion? What is meant by that?
2. Has your experience of Church been one of fellowship, sharing, communion, *koinonia*? Does the Church come through to you as the mystery of *life*? How do we fail in living up to that ideal?

3. I grew up to associate 'fellowship' with Protestant terminology. Perhaps that has something to say of the quality of (my) Catholic worship and community involvement. Have other Christian traditions acquitted themselves better in this regard?
4. What lessons can we learn from the Fathers—Irenaeus, Cyprian, Augustine—about respecting the claim of other Christians to communion with us despite the different positions they arrive at in their theology and life? Is our Church situation much different in this regard from the early Church?
5. Does communion in the Eucharist prove to be a private thing for me, or does it lead me on to 'actively participate in the ongoing restoration of the world's situation and the human condition' (W.C.C.'s Lima document)? How can I make this connection real, as the early Church did?

3

MYSTERY AND KINGDOM

It is the contention of this book that the Church is understood most adequately as the mystery of Christ, the divine plan for all things that brings us a share in God's own life as a graced community. This theology of Church does most justice to the whole biblical message, and is supported by comment from the Fathers. Understandably, then, the Christian Church's efforts at self-definition in recent decades of this century have accentuated these themes, and they have received support in some theological writing.

That this accent in theology and magisterium has not been consistent is due partly to the diversity of the biblical message itself, as well as to our growth in its understanding. Developments in biblical and patristic studies have highlighted scriptural ways of perceiving and presenting Church; priority among these has taken time to emerge. We have given attention, for example, to Pauline and Johannine ecclesiology, with reference also to sapiential theology from the Old Testament.

The teaching of Jesus

What has loomed less large has been Jesus' own teaching from the Gospels, and this may seem an anomaly. In fact, Jesus does not give much specific mention to Church as such in our Gospels, something that has given rise to questioning and comment. Hans Küng warns us not to take as cynical the verdict of Alfred Loisy at the turn of the century, 'Jesus proclaimed the kingdom of God, and what came was the Church'.[1] There is certainly no doubt of the centrality in Jesus' teaching (at least as far as the Synoptic Gospels record it) of this notion of *basileia*, for which 'kingdom' is, as we have noted, generally an unhappy translation. The emphasis falls there from the first moment of the Galilean ministry in verse 14 of Mark's first chapter: 'Jesus came into Galilee, preaching the gospel of God, and saying, "The time is fulfilled, and the *basileia* of God is at hand; repent, and believe in the Gospel."'

Jesus is saying, over and over again in the Synoptic Gospels, that he has come, in the line of Yahweh, the enthroned king of Old Testament psalms and prophets, to implement a reign of justice and love. It is this reign, this value system, that Jesus in his person, by his acts of healing and in his teaching, particularly the Beatitudes and the parables, brings to the fore. Ernst Käsemann, whom we have also seen is suspicious of attempts to find fully-fledged ecclesiologies in the New Testament, says:

> Jesus regarded it as his task and as the grace given to him to witness to the gracious God as present and as breaking into the world. His approach to his task resembled that of the Old Testament prophets: he interpreted his own message and his personal advent as the beginning of the divine activity, just as, according to *Mt* 11:12, the proclamation of the *basileia* at hand is itself the proximity of this *basileia*. Thus he enters on his proclamatory function as, so to speak, the incarnation of the divine promise.[2]

Käsemann and Loisy remind us there is no reference to Church in this proclamation of *basileia*. Their case is strengthened when we consider the movement within the New Testament itself to identify the *basileia* with Jesus: where *Mk* 11:10 says, 'Blessed is the *basileia* of our father David that is coming', the saying has become 'Hosanna to the Son of David! Blessed is he who comes...' (*Mt* 21:9). Raymond Brown further notes the movement in John from *basileia*, which occurs at only two places in that Gospel, to the *basileus*, king, himself: 'The Synoptic emphasis on the *basileia* making itself felt in Jesus seems to have become in John an emphasis on Jesus who is *basileus* and who reigns... The parables that the Synoptics associate with the *basileia* seem to give way in John to figurative speech centred about the person of Jesus.'[3] On the other hand, there is an opposite tendency in the New Testament to reify and localise the *basileia* in the sense of 'kingdom' (as in the Growth parables): one enters it; there are keys to it. Brown comments, 'The kingdom and the church have begun to be partially identified',[4] though the Lutheran exegete and the Modernist priest would still not agree.

Relating Church to *basileia*

The result of this diverse New Testament statement has been a range of attempts to formulate the relationship between Church and *basileia*, some commencing from an inadequate understanding of the Greek term, evidenced usually by their option for 'kingdom' as a translation. A feature of many of these definitions is that *basileia* is seen as an eschatological reality and the Church is its present, this-worldly realisation. The Fathers of Vatican II spoke this way; they began, in *Lumen Gentium* 5[5], by stating that Jesus came to preach the *regnum* (in the Fathers' Latin), to confirm it in his miracles and in particular to make it visible in his person; they could then speak of 'the Church, or, in other words, the *regnum* of Christ now present in mystery'[6]. Likewise, in the Constitution on the Church in the Modern World they say, 'On this earth the *regnum* is already present in mystery; at the Lord's coming it will reach its completion'.[7] The 1985 Synod sees the Church pressing onwards towards the kingdom of the future.[8]

Many theologians can be found speaking similarly, even if exegetes are generally agreed that Synoptic emphasis in *basileia* is primarily on the present dynamic activity of Jesus in whom God's reign has come. The Growth parables, we have noted, represent a rather marginal development of this. So Jürgen Moltmann says, 'The Church in the power of the Spirit is not yet the kingdom of God, but it is its anticipation in history'.[9] The phrase is echoed in Catholic Hans Küng,[10] Protestant Jan Lochman,[11] Orthodox Dumitru Staniloae.[12] Others, respecting perhaps the realised eschatology of the Synoptic *basileia* or just out of touch with the biblical data, would identify Church and kingdom here and now.[13]

The challenge for us is rather to relate Jesus' statement on God's *basileia* in the Gospels with that comprehensive biblical ecclesiology of the mystery of Christ. We have found this developed particularly in the Pauline letters, and the proto-Pauline material in the New Testament predates the Gospels by at least several decades. Yet it is not in terms of mystery that Jesus speaks in the later Synoptic Gospels but in terms of the *basileia* of God (or, in Matthew's euphemism, of heaven). Only at *Mark* 4:11 does *mysterion* occur, and there in association with *basileia*, in a passage which Matthew and Luke hasten to modify so as to alter drastically the sense of Jesus' words. We need to look closely at this passage, for it helps us to grasp the meaning of *basileia* in Jesus' mouth and to relate it both to mystery and to Church.[14]

The mystery of the *basileia*

The verse occurs in Mark's account of the Galilean ministry of Jesus. Beside the lake he 'taught them many things in parables,' including the parable of the sower. The text goes on:

> (10) When he was alone, those around him with the Twelve asked him about the parables. (11) He said to them, 'To you the *mysterion* of God's *basileia* has been given, whereas to those others outside everything is in parables, (12) so that "looking they may look and not see, and hearing they may hear and not understand, lest they be converted and forgiven".' (13) He said to them, 'Don't you understand this parable? How will you grasp all the parables? (14) The sower sows the word...'

There are some unusual features of this passage that suggest it represents a collection of sayings from different parts of the ministry. Commentators point to atypical vocabulary and style and the 'intolerable' statement of the purpose of parables that results; they draw attention to the fact that verses 11–12 do not take up the question in verse 10, which is only answered in verse 14; verse 13 indicates the disciples do *not* understand the parable and thus contradicts vv.11–12.

Strangely, Matthew and Luke do nothing about these difficulties in the whole passage. Instead, they concentrate on altering Mark's version of verse 11 as though it is shocking. Where Mark says the disciples (we) have been granted a share in the mystery, the great sacred reality, which is God's reign (in the person of Jesus), the other evangelists identically reduce this wonderful gift to a 'cognitive experience'[15] by reading, 'To you it has been permitted to know the mysteries of the *basileia*', inserting the verb 'to know', changing mystery to the plural (which we have seen gives a completely different sense), and using the verb 'give' in the sense 'permit' uniquely at this place. They are desperate, for reasons we shall see, to avoid the sense intended by Mark, and they have succeeded in losing the wonderful effect of his collocation of *mysterion* and *basileia* and his consequent suggestion of our share in the great reality of God's reign coming in Jesus' person. It is a truly rich meaning, which the early Church seized upon: Origen, the great catechist, was prompted to coin the term *autobasileia* for Jesus, who incorporated in himself all the values of God's reign;[16] Tertullian at the end of the second century quotes with approval Marcion's saying (no heresy in this), 'In the Gospel Christ himself is God's *regnum*.'[17]

Modern commentators too, at least those who escape a facile translation of these two Greek terms, recognise the significance of Mark's version of Jesus' saying, which had not originally (it seems) any reference to interpreting parables. 'In Ch 4:11 Jesus was not thinking of the Kingdom of God in any abstract sense, whether as a future or a present reality, but of the Kingdom as it is embodied in his own purpose.'[18] 'Mark indeed presupposes an age-long purpose of God, which he traces back to the beginning of creation (10:6; 13:19) a phrase which—not incidentally—Mark shares with *Dan* 12:1.'[19]

In fact, as we said at the outset of this chapter, Jesus in the Gospels does not spend much time meditating on that 'age-long purpose of God' which Paul spoke of often as the mystery of Christ. He both represents and announces the in-breaking into history of God's power, kingship, at that particular period within the overall design. Paul's accent was on the historical, biblical and cosmic dimensions of that design; of Jesus' ministry he says nothing before the Supper, though the Paschal Mystery of Jesus he sees as the focal point of the eternal plan which for him is Christ. Mark, in referring uniquely to the mystery, has been thought by his classic commentator to be under Paul's influence.[20] The Church as mystery is not therefore an explicit theme in Jesus' teaching in the Synoptic Gospels. For the Church as *koinonia*, too, we found ourselves turning rather to the Gospel and Letters of John.

A shift of emphasis

There clearly has been a shift of emphasis from the Pauline sweep of history to the Synoptic centring on the ministry of Jesus. It is something of a movement from the Christ of faith back to the Jesus of history. This direction is contrary to what we might have expected. Käsemann comments that the movement from Paul to the Gospels reverses the usual movement in the history of religion whereby the preacher becomes the object of preaching, and such reversal in the Gospels constitutes 'the most interesting and theologically important happening in primitive Christianity'.[21] It also perhaps retarded development of New Testament ecclesiology. James Dunn, too, sees the Gospels as a corrective: 'Initially interest in the earthly teaching and ministry of Jesus was subordinate to the parousia hope, and the Jesus-tradition served in part at first as a kind of counterbalance to (over)enthusiastic imminent expectation.'[22]

An effect of this reversal was to highlight the challenge of Jesus and his message. 'Jesus is in his own person the challenge to decision', says Küng. 'His Gospel is the last word of God before the end, the urgent call to unavoidable and radical decision for God and his reign. The hour of decision is not at some vague time in the future, but *now*.'[23] The challenge of God and his *basileia* is presented by the Jesus of the Gospels particularly in the parables and, as we have seen in *Mk* 4, Jesus' challenge was not always met. Did Jesus lament only a failure to understand? Or was it a failure to respond to the challenge, the challenge of the *basileia* and/or the *basileus* himself? Brown, when dealing with the parable of the sheepgate (*Jn* 10:6), agrees that 'the failure is not primarily an intellectual problem; it is an unwillingness to respond to the challenge of the parables'[24] centred on the *basileia* in the Synoptics, centring on Jesus in John. Mark's saying in 4:11 retains this focus for the challenge; Matthew's and Luke's adaptation loses that focus to make it a merely intellectual failure.

Why did they abandon the association of *basileia* with *mysterion*, lose the sense of that word by turning it to the plural, and introduce a verb denoting a merely cognitive experience? What was so shocking about the dominical saying in the form in which Mark preserved it? Commentators we have quoted suggest that Christianity after Paul felt the need to bring post-Easter enthusiasm back to pre-Easter history; Rudolf Bultmann says that, unlike Mark's tolerance of a 'mythical element', in Matthew and Luke 'the Christ myth recedes in favour of the picture of the earthly ministry of Jesus'.[25] The Pauline mystery, so rich for a comprehensive ecclesiology, especially for the Gentile outreach, was less palatable for writers with a less universalist viewpoint (it is significant that some manuscripts of Luke do retain *mysterion*); the cosmic dimensions of the mystery were even less acceptable.

In a sense, then, the note of regret that is suggested by Loisy's statement should be expressed in the reverse order, as far as the formation of the New Testament is concerned: first came a theology of Church (in Paul) capable of dealing with the universal scope of God's plan, and the later trend was to highlight Jesus' preaching of the *basileia*. What is lost is the Pauline notion of church as mystery growing into Christ's body: the mystery of Christ is also the body of Christ. Käsemann explains:

The theme—which may go well back behind Paul—of

> the Church as the body of Christ is a precise expression of a relevant theology for the very reason that it emphasises better than any other conception of the Church the world-wide nature of a Christianity which is breaking through to the Gentile mission and the universality of the redemptive happening which this break-through indicates.[26]

Significance of *basileia* for Church

If that is lost, what is gained for our understanding of Church from the focus on *basileia* (a term not frequent in Paul's mouth[27])? We have seen that Jesus expected people to respond to the challenge of his person and the challenge of his teaching. A gift had been given: that is the thrust of *Mk* 4:11, 'To you has been given a share in the mystery that is God's reign [in me],' and in its present context a reproach is implied for failure to respond. We are expected to accept an invitation to live and work according to the value system that is *basileia* (phrases like 'work for the Kingdom' being less helpful). We may say that Jesus intended that his Church would grow into the *basileia* he desiderated. Jan Lochman says:

> It makes all the difference to any civilisation and society if there are within it groups of human beings who, in face of the tribulations of their time, keep their eyes steadily on the kingdom of God by praying for its coming, by being its disciples, especially in the direction indicated by Christ's promises: advocating the cause of the poor, serving prisoners and the disabled, raising up the oppressed and broken, and, above all, proclaiming the 'acceptable year of the Lord', God's liberating future. These groups of witnesses of the kingdom of God who try to 'love both earth and God at the same time' are Christians (although not exclusively so), the pilgrim people of God, the church.[28]

Vatican II tries briefly to tie together the two approaches to Church, mystery and kingdom: 'The mystery of holy Church is made clear in her very foundation: the Lord Jesus made a beginning to his Church by preaching the good news, namely, the coming of God's *regnum* promised for ages in the Scriptures.'[29] The collocation of the two is not an explanation, nor is the further statement of the Church as '*regnum* already present in mystery'. Council documents cannot perhaps be expected to supply the background of the key terms involved, and doubtless the Council Fathers were not clear about it. We know enough, however, to enable us to confirm the accuracy of that identification. Within that eternal divine plan for our share in divine life, a plan we call the mystery of Christ and recognise in its community dimension as the Church, Jesus comes to inaugurate and preach God's reign and eminently achieve it in his Paschal Mystery, a point on which all the Gospels and Paul are in complete agreement. The invitation to participate in that design, to accept the offer of life, and to work for the realisation of that divine rule is issued to all people. Acceptance of the invitation not only constitutes membership of the Church but also commits one to the welfare of God's world as a whole, just as Jesus' works and signs, in the manner of the Old Testament divine King, extended to inanimate nature as well. A further chapter will therefore be addressed to the mystery beyond the Church; the more tantalising relationship is not so much between Church and 'kingdom' as between Church and world.

Points for discussion

1. Why is it, do you think that 'Church' is so infrequently on the lips of Jesus in the Gospels? (Consult a concordance for details of this Gospel usage by comparison with the rest of the New Testament.)
2. By contrast, Jesus is always speaking of *basileia* in the Synoptic Gospels. What picture do we get there of the relation between *basileia* and Church? What is the danger of identifying the two (as of opposing them)? How do you see the Church fulfilling Jesus' ideals in *basileia* (as in the Beatitudes, for instance)?
3. In the third century, the great Alexandrian scholar-catechist Origen spoke of Jesus as the *autobasileia*,

thus grasping the sense of that critical Gospel passage *Mk* 4:11. What was lost by the reshaping of that dominical saying in *Mt* and *Lk*?

4. Do you think people understand the Gospel notion of *basileia* when translated as it usually is by 'kingdom'? Are phrases like 'working for the kingdom', 'children of the kingdom' helpful, or overly vague? (Are people's understandings of 'Church' any clearer, for that matter?)

4

THE MYSTERY BEYOND THE CHURCH

In the beautiful hymn of thanksgiving opening the letter to the Ephesians, the purpose of the mystery of Christ is stated as a plan for the fulness of time to sum up/bring together/cap off all things in him, things in heaven and things on earth (1:10). The Greek verb in the sentence is applied metaphorically, deriving from the process of setting a keystone in place in the construction of an arch, and it may thus also be used in rhetoric to describe a final summary of an argument, as Paul does in *Rom* 13:9. Its application in this letter to the consummation of the divine design is most appropriate. What is also notable in the verse is the repetition of the neuter 'things': the mystery of Christ embraces the whole of creation, not simply its human beneficiaries.

We have seen evangelists shrinking from this accent on the cosmic dimensions of the mystery in their treatment of a dominical saying, so that the word *mysterion* never occurs again in the Gospels. In fact, in the biblical message as a whole the relevance, welfare and eventual destiny of the created world is definitely in a minor key. It is the salvation of the people (and not even all of them) that is in focus for most of the Bible; even in the New Testament Jesus' mission from the outset is given this limited scope: 'Call him Jesus [= Yahweh saves], for he shall save his people from their sins' (*Mt* 1:21). And this narrowing of focus is predictable, considering the composers of our text, with all their limitations and prejudices.

Thankfully, then, we have also in both Old and New Testaments composers who were able to extend their horizons further to consider all of God's creation in their view of the divine plan. In the Old Testament it is the psalmists and particularly the Wisdom writers to whom credit goes for this; these sages not only looked beyond one chosen people to consider all humanity, good and evil, they not only extended the scope of salvation history to draw it back beyond the patriarchs to the beginnings of the world and forward beyond the grave to everlasting life with God, but they also took a serious interest in material creation as well.[1] The psalms in some places show this latter interest, as do the creation narratives in *Genesis*. But they are concerns not close to the heart of historical and prophetic composers, and are thus often ignored also by biblical theologians.

In the New Testament it is almost solely Paul who gives formal attention to the place of the whole world within the divine plan, even if Jesus in his manner of teaching resembles the down-to-earth sages; the evangelists prefer to follow him in his nominated role of saving his people from their sins, and other New Testament authors study dogmatic and moral implications of this for the Christian life. Paul is interested in wisdom as God's comprehensive plan, as we have seen above, in Christ as the wisdom and power of God, in the overarching mystery of Christ, in the stance of Christians towards a world the form of which is passing away (1 *Cor* 7:31) and in the process by which all creation escapes its present confines to reach a goal awaiting it as one awaits us:

> In my reckoning, whatever we are called upon to suffer in this present time cannot compare with the glory which is going to burst upon us. For the whole created universe eagerly and expectantly awaits the day when God will show the world who his sons are. For the whole created universe was involved in a process of meaningless frustration, not of its own choice, but by the decree of God who did so subject it. But the situation was never hopeless, because even the created universe itself will be liberated from its servitude to death's decay, and will come to enjoy the glorious liberty of the children of God. For we know that up to now the whole created universe groans in all its parts, like a woman in the birthpangs. This is

> not only true of the created universe. We too, even although we have received in the Spirit a foretaste of what the new life will be like, groan inwardly, as we wait longingly for God to complete his adoption of us, so that we will be emancipated from sin, both body and soul (*Rom* 8:18–23).[2]

Paul is short on detail in this picture of our sharing the eschaton with the rest of creation, as we share the present times; visionary, apocalyptic writing is like this. But the great value of the apostle's and sages' insights is that they maintain a balance, one that is ever in peril because of our reluctance to consider their emphasis. We, with a natural prejudice characterising also the biblical composers, fix our attention on the human beneficiaries of the mystery of Christ—ourselves. We tend to ignore or downplay the place of the world in this economy. Our view thus becomes dualist instead of displaying a Pauline, sapiential integrity. Even before Christianity, of course, people had difficulty seeing the unity in any divine plan; dualism was rife in pagan cosmologies (as the book of *Wisdom* confirms). With the Incarnation, people were not well equipped to deal with the challenge of the God-man, and early Christological aberrations swung to one extreme or the other. As Johannes Metz says, 'It could be shown that it was an unchristian conception of the world that was chiefly behind the Christological heresies of the early Church.'[3]

Church versus world

Because of this lack of an integral understanding of the mystery of Christ and a dualist approach to the human and other beneficiaries of the plan, problems arise also concerning the place of the Church within the divine plan and in particular concerning its relations with the world. The Bible as a whole, we have seen, chooses not to deal in detail with the *koinonia*, fellowship, participation that all other created things enjoy with the Creator, and yet as created and existing things they plainly exemplify in their own way such participation. Students of the Bible have endorsed this unbalanced option, though shaken at times by such challenging movements as the contemporary conservation lobby groups, who by their insistence have encouraged us to look more closely at recent archeological evidence on the biblical statement of human creation 'in God's image and likeness' and consequent human responsibility for the universe.

Because of this dualistic imbalance the world is seen as the enemy of the Church or a threat to it. 'Twenty centuries of history bear witness to the fact that balance between the two is almost impossible to come by,' says De Lubac in writing on 'The Church in the world,'[4] though dealing specifically with an ecclesiology that sees the Church as perfect society in competition with civil society. The problem does, in fact, arise from a failure to align ecclesiology with the total mystery of Christ. Its roots, beyond this longstanding dualism, go back in Christian literature to the two cities of *Hebrews* and Augustine; whatever of the truth that 'we have not here a lasting city but seek one that is to come' (*Heb* 13:14), there is already explicit here only a dualist incompatibility. Strangely Vatican II, in trying to come to terms with those twenty centuries of imbalance in its Pastoral Constitution on the Church in the Modern World, raises again the two cities analogy.[5] Still, the Constitution does attack formally the 'split between the faith which many people profess and their daily lives' as well as 'any false opposition between their professional and social activities, on the one hand, and their religious life on the other'. It also speaks of the Church's indebtedness to the modern world.[6]

Twenty-five years later, however, the Church at that level thought the Council had moved too far against a dualistic view of the divine plan. The 1985 Synod chose to distance itself from the Council's optimism based on God's acceptance of the world in the Incarnation: its stress, in the light of that intervening quarter century, fell rather on more negative features of the world, and the bishops thought reference to the cross of Jesus more appropriate:

The signs of our times do not exactly coincide, in some points, with those of the time of the Council. From among these special attention must be paid to the phenomenon of secularism. The Council certainly did affirm the legitimate autonomy of temporal realities [cf. *Gaudium et Spes* 36 and elsewhere]. In this sense a correctly understood secularisation must be admitted. But totally different is that secularism that consists of an autonomous vision of man and the world, one which leaves aside the dimension of mystery, indeed neglects and denies it. This immanentism is a reduction of the integral vision of man, a reduction which does not lead to his true liberation but to a new idolatry, to the slavery of ideologies, to a life in the narrow and often oppressive structures of this world.[7]

Today there is a worldwide escalation of hunger, oppression, injustice and war, torment and terrorism and all kinds of violence. This impels us to a new and deeper theological reflection in order to interpret such signs in the light of the Gospel. It seems to us that in the difficulties of our day God wishes to teach us more deeply the value, the importance and the centrality of the cross of Jesus Christ. Therefore the relationship between human history and salvation history is to be explained in the light of the Paschal Mystery. Certainly the theology of the cross does not at all exclude the theology of the creation and incarnation, but, as is clear, it presupposes it.[8]

Midway between Council and Synod, in 1975, Pope Paul VI had tried to maintain the optimism and balance of *Gaudium et Spes* in his apostolic exhortation *Evangelii Nuntiandi* following the previous year's Synod on evangelisation in the modern world. In this remarkably serene document he spoke clearly and positively (unlike the above brief concession) about 'secularisation, which is the effort, in itself just and legitimate and in no way incompatible with faith or religion, to discover in creation, in each thing or each happening in the universe, the laws which regulate them with a certain autonomy, but with the inner conviction that the Creator has placed these laws there'.[9] Only then does he warn of a godless secularism.

What is perhaps missing above is the admission and acceptance of the world and the autonomy of secular realities in the light of the mysteries of creation and incarnation, just as the whole world should acknowledge the legitimate place of the Church (properly understood as mystery). Again it is a question of that biblical, or at least sapiential and Pauline, balance. Antagonism, opposition on the one side almost merits a like response on the other—that the Church should be considered irrelevant. Fortunately, there are authoritative statements, like *Gaudium et Spes* and *Evangelii Nuntiandi*, and theological investigations upholding a less inimical relationship between Church and world within a total view of the mystery of Christ.

Someone brought face to face with the effects of that hostile, unaccepting relationship was Dietrich Bonhoeffer, theologian of the Confessing Church in Hitler's Germany, imprisoned in Buchenwald during the days of allied bombing, the Normandy invasion and abortive attempt on Hitler's life, and finally hanged. In his *Letters and Papers from Prison* he expresses his disgust at the inhumanity of man to man and the minimal impact of religion on captives and captors alike. For this he blamed himself and his fellow churchmen for their failure to come to grips with the critical relationship of Church and world:

> The attack by Christian apologetic upon the adulthood of the world I consider to be in the first place pointless, in the second ignoble, and in the third un-Christian.[10]

> During these years the Church has fought for self-preservation as though it were an end in itself, and has thereby lost its chance to speak a word of reconciliation to mankind and the world at large.[11]

Though never shaken in his beliefs and Christian practices in this squalid environment, he was forced to contemplate the prospect of a Churchless world or at least, in his oft quoted phrase, 'a religionless Christianity'. His diary entries show him grappling with the critical balance:

> The thing that keeps coming back to me is, what *is* Christianity, and indeed what *is* Christ for us today? ... We are proceeding towards a time of no religion at

all: men as they are now cannot be religious any more. Even those who honestly describe themselves as 'religious' do not in least act up to it, and so when they say 'religious' they evidently mean something quite different...

How can Christ become the Lord even of those with no religion? If religion is no more than the garment of Christianity—and even that garment has had very different aspects at different periods—then what is a religionless Christianity?[12]

The place of religion is taken by the Church—that is, in itself, as the Bible teaches it should be—but the world is made to depend upon itself and left to its own devices, and that is all wrong.[13]

Church and world

Bonhoeffer did not despair of the future of the Church, but before dying he forecast its different stance before the world. The change in attitude he desiderated is evident in the statements of the Catholic community's Council two decades later, where there is an attempt to clarify the meaning of 'world' and articulate a balanced relationship with Church:

> God's plan for the world is that people should strive together to restore the order of things of this world and constantly develop it. The things of this world include the good things of this life and the family, culture, economic affairs, arts and professions, political institutions, international relations and other things of this kind as well as their development and progress. All these are not only aids to the human being's final end but have their own value implanted in them by God, whether considered in themselves or as part of the whole order of this world.[14]

The things of this world, 'the temporal order', are seen as good not only in themselves, but also as related to the human person, and finally as falling within the mystery of Christ that gathers together all things—though 'this does not deprive them of their own independence, goals, laws and resources'.

Paul and the Wisdom writers would be happy with this statement of the goodness of all creation, as they would with the statements in *Gaudium et Spes* acknowledging the mutually beneficial relationship of Church and world and the condemnation of false oppositions.[15] The Council texts are also indebted to those Fathers of the Church who pondered this relationship, like Irenaeus and Justin as early as the second century. More recent inspiration came from thinkers like Teilhard de Chardin, who endeavoured to put together the experience of a paleontologist with Pauline apocalyptic, Karl Rahner and Yves Congar, who had all written in this vein in the years before the Council.

For Rahner, our living at 'the end of the ages', that is, since the coming of Christ, makes a difference for Christians' approach to a world now free of myth:

> It is absolutely legitimate to regard this new period as one whose ultimate reason is to be found in the faith of Christianity. For the demythologisation and secularisation of the world which not only actually takes place but is willed and carried out by Christianity has turned the world into a material which man himself can manipulate technologically; and only through the Christian message concerning the final self-transcendence of the spirit by grace into an absolute God who is totally distinct from the created world, has cosmocentricity been turned into an anthropocentricity. Viewed in this light, it is perhaps meaningful and understandable that the Incarnation stands at the beginning of this first really all-human period.[16]

For Rahner, as for *Gaudium et Spes*, it is in the Incarnation that God again accepts the world for what it is and sets it free. Johannes Metz also sees the Incarnation enabling the Church to accept a world freed of myth and to assist in the demythologising process:

> In our secular world today new forms of myth are emerging. And like every myth they have something about them that is violent, constructed, unfree. They—and not actually the secularity of the world—are the real danger of our situation of faith and the misfor-

tune of our times. In contrast, the Christian appears as the truly secular man—for only he is prepared to let the secular sphere be itself, through his imitation in faith of that more profound acceptance out of which all that is secular about the world draws its life, its liberating acceptance through God and Jesus Christ.[17]

These writers are at pains to recommend on the part of Christians acceptance of the secularity of secular things; but it is a liberating acceptance, not a mere submission of the spiritual to the material. If one can speak, as Bonhoeffer does, of the 'true worldliness' of the Christian, one can also speak, as the New Testament does, of renunciation of the world and of repentance and conversion in confronting it, as Jesus does in announcing the *basileia* at *Mk* 1:14: 'The *basileia* is at hand; repent!' Jan Lochman, who points out that Luke's parallel launching of Jesus' ministry is couched in terms of liberation from oppression (*Lk* 4:18–19), stresses the appropriateness of this response of conversion to the coming of the *basileia*: 'The potentialities and powers invested in the creation and in humanity as part of this creation are turned by our human rebellion against the Creator into false absolutes and are even absolutized in opposition to humanity... It is to this sombre background that the prayer for the coming of God's kingdom is related; it is into this dark abyss that it reaches. In this respect it is the first step of conversion and, in this sense, really the one thing needful.'[18]

Acceptance of the true worldliness of the world, on the paradigm of the Incarnation, is thus utterly compatible with repentance, conversion, renunciation of the world in the hope of the final realisation of all that *basileia* involves; on this basis the human beneficiaries of the mystery of Christ—the Church—accept and respect the place in the mystery of all else that God has created, all else that shares in the divine *koinonia* in its own way.

The Christian is moved to flee and to renounce the world not because he despises the world but because he hopes in the future of the world as proclaimed in God's promises. And this hope gives him a responsibility for the world and its future—a future from which we can too often isolate ourselves in forms of presumption and despair... The Church is not the goal of her own strivings; this goal is the Kingdom of God. The Church always lives in a certain sense from the proclamation of her provisional character and from her historically progressive surrender to the coming Kingdom of God.[19]

The difference between the Christian hope of resurrection and a mythological hope is that the Christian hope sends a man to his life on earth in a wholly new way which is even more sharply defined than it is in the Old Testament. The Christian, unlike the devotees of the salvation myths, does not need a last refuge in the eternal from earthly tasks and difficulties.[20]

Church for world

As we forecast above, a truly adequate understanding of the mystery of Christ, of the biblical *koinonia*, of Jesus' incorporation and demonstration of the *basileia* would bring us to an adequate understanding of the relation between Church and world. These terms have repeatedly surfaced in the efforts of those attempting to deal with that relationship. Far from being a relationship of antithesis and opposition, it is appearing in the light of the biblical intuitions to be one of mutuality and even service; the Church is for the world, whether seen as it is or as what it is to become.

For Johannes Metz the Church alone can guarantee that the world escapes the falsifying myths of sin to achieve true worldliness: 'Grace perfects the true worldliness of the world. And that is why the Church, or the historically tangible sign and the institution of this grace within the world, is not the opponent but the guarantor of the world. The Church exists for the sake of the world. For (to rephrase a well-known saying) the world is the end of the ways of God. The Church itself is in the service of the universal will of God for the world.'[21] (In this reference to God's will for the world we recognise Paul's thinking on mystery, purpose, will, wisdom.) From this point of view we can appreciate the deferential remarks of Pope Paul VI on the Church's role of service to the world (and of all those who write on a servant model of Church):[22]

> We will strive, so far as our weakness permits and God gives us the grace, to approach the world in which God has destined us to live. We will approach it with reverence, persistence and love, in an effort to get to know it and to offer it the gifts of truth and grace of which God has made us the custodian. We will strive to make the world share in the divine redemption and in the hope which inspires us. Engraven on our heart are those words of Christ which we would humbly but resolutely make our own, 'For God sent the Son into the world, not to condemn the world, but that the world might be saved through him' (*Jn* 3:17).[23]

In the wake of Paul VI's encyclical, *Gaudium et Spes* also spoke of the Church's responsibility for the world—and not simply for its human inhabitants, as that Johannine *kosmos* quoted by the Pope could be interpreted to mean. Elsewhere Vatican II spoke of the Church as the sacrament of the world's salvation. The World Council of Churches at Vancouver in 1983 expressed itself in similar terms: 'It is only a church which goes out from its eucharistic centre, strengthened by word and sacrament, and thus strengthened in its own identity, resolved to become what it is, that can take the world on to its own agenda.'[24] Hopefully in these statements Paul's 'whole of creation' is in mind; otherwise, relationship and service of Church to world is only partial. For Congar there is no doubt: he can speak of the hypostatic or personal dignity the universe attains to by its relationship to the human being, bringing the cosmos to its own proper goal.[25]

> In God's unitary design the Church and the world are both ordered to this kingdom in the end, but by different ways and on different accounts. Church and world have the same end, but only the same ultimate end. That they should have the same end is due to God's unitary plan and to the fact that the whole cosmos is united with man in a shared destiny. That they

should have only the same ultimate end prevents a confusion that would be bad for the Church, as raising a risk of dissolving her own proper mission in that of history, and bad for the world, as raising a risk of misunderstanding and hindering its own proper development.[26]

Congar can speak like this because he thinks in terms of 'God's unitary plan', the mystery of Christ. That this thinking is germane to Orthodox theology as well appears from the statement on the Church arrived at by the joint commission of Catholic and Orthodox Churches in Munich in 1982: 'To speak of the sacramental nature of the mystery of Christ is to bring to mind the possibility given to man, and through him to the whole cosmos, to experience the 'new creation', the kingdom of God here and now through material and created realities.'[27]

So the Church's service of the world is not simply to guarantee its true worldliness but also to transform it and ensure it reaches the end intended in God's *basileia*. Jürgen Moltmann says:

> For this reason 'Church for the world' can mean nothing else but 'Church for the kingdom of God' and the renewing of the world... The whole body of Christians is engaged in the apostolate of hope for the world and finds therein its essence—namely, that which makes it the Church of God. It is not in itself the salvation of the world, so that the 'churchifying' of the world would mean the latter's salvation, but it serves the coming salvation of the world and is like an arrow sent out into the world to point to the future.[28]

Much more work has obviously to be done on this subject of the role of the Church for the world; the Bible, we said, is more interested in the challenge of 'saving people from their sins'. As has been suggested already, there is a similar tentativeness about some endeavours, evident in their restricting the world to its human inhabitants. There is truth in that, but only partial truth; that is why the Pauline concept of the mystery of Christ, 'God's unitary design' in Congar's phrase, is so illuminating in being adequate, and adequacy is needed in this area. Paul spoke plainly of *pasa ktisis*, all created realities. And yet he spoke only in a flash of insight there in *Romans* 8, without specifying details of the glorious process of delivery and deliverance of the world and its achievement of an end it shares with us. He is short on detail elsewhere, too, as at 1 *Cor* 7:31 when recommending Christian detachment as a recipe for life in a world whose 'form is passing away', being transformed (not annihilated). We need to think more on how we the Church assist the world in this process of transformation.

Emphasis on God's unitary design, the mystery of Christ, can perhaps lead us even further, into seeing not simply Church *for* world but Church *including* world. For this more daring vision flashes of insight are even rarer. De Lubac quotes an eminent authority: 'Following in the footsteps of St Thomas, we can give the name 'Church' to that gigantic organism which includes all the host of the angels as well as men, and even extends to the whole of the cosmos as well.'[29] Metz, reflecting Congar's accent on unity in the manner of the Pauline mystery, brings Church and world together, allowing only an accidental reason for the Church's separate existence:

> The Church must be understood within the framework of the universal will of God for the world. God is concerned with the world, not really with the Church as different from the world. Only because the loving acceptance of the world by God was rejected and protested by the world did the 'Church' come into being at all (as distinct from the 'world')—as a sign and guarantee of the ultimate victory of God in relation to the world, which resisted him and, falling victim to itself in sin, also missed finding its own being. Hence the Church must always *also* be seen as that provisional thing that it is in salvation history (and which finally falls back again on the world itself).[30]

A profound insight into the divine design, reminiscent of Augustine's terse statement, 'The Church is the world, reconciled' (whereas 'the world unreconciled is everything apart from the Church').[31]

Conclusion

Perhaps at this point, in attempting to plumb the mystery beyond the Church, mere theology (even if 'a certain participation in God's own knowledge of himself', in St Thomas's view)[32] falters, to give way to mysticism. Better to follow Paul in his conclusion to the survey of the many-faceted mystery of Christ in *Romans* 9–11 and admit the overwhelming beauty and immensity of the divine design:

> O the depth of the riches and wisdom and knowledge of God! How unsearchable are his judgements and how inscrutable his ways! For from him and through him and to him are all things. To him be glory forever. Amen (*Rom* 11:33, 36).

The full dimensions of the mystery, which under one aspect is the Church, are simply breathtaking; Paul could only marvel and worship—a model for us. In our respect for divine transcendence, however, let us imitate the balance of the East and marvel as well at divine immanence. God has placed the Church in his world with a responsibility and salvific role for it. Where there is responsibility there can be no apartheid, nor is there excuse for it on the false grounds of some opposition, some pagan dualism, between Church and world. Creation and Incarnation have accepted and blessed the world; for Redemption it awaits the caring ministration of us, the Church. As we offer life to one another in the unfolding of this mystery, so we must work to achieve the purpose God has for his world, freeing it from enslavement, exploitation and a false adulation. Worldly involvement and yet detachment will right Adam's wrong and free the world 'from its bondage to decay and obtain the glorious liberty of the children of God' (*Rom* 8:21).

Points for discussion

1. Do we have difficulty seeing a place in God's plan for material things, occupations, interests, activities? Are these considered irrelevant when we theologise about the mystery of Christ? Can we be guilty of the kind of

dualism about creation that characterised pagan myths?

2. 'We have not here a lasting city but seek one that is to come', said the epistle to the Hebrews; Augustine wrote an influential work on *The City of God.* Does the two cities analogy help us in relating our life in the Church and life in the world, or does it foster dualism? What did Vatican II have to say (in *Gaudium et Spes*, for example)?
3. Secularity, secularisation, secularism: the terms have appeared in magisterial statements over the past few decades, manifesting a concern with the relation between Church and world. Have these statements been marked by clarity and consistency, or can you detect changes in position by teachers within the Church on this critical relationship?
4. 'The Church exists for the sake of the world.' Would you agree with Johannes Metz that the Church, far from being in opposition to the world, is there to serve it and indeed guarantee its true worldliness? How does the Church do this, in practice?

5

MYSTERY, MODELS, IMAGES, FIGURES

The mystery of Christ, which is the Church, is a thing of great and varied beauty, displaying various dimensions—biblical, historical, personal, even cosmic—that can be appreciated at different times. In the Pauline letters, attempts to grapple with the mystery result in a range of other terms to do it justice—will, purpose, plan, wisdom. The mystery is described as manifold, many-faceted, multicoloured. The New Testament authors borrow terminology from the Greek Bible to meet the challenge. Using a term that occurs, significantly, in *Genesis* 37 of the coat made for Joseph by his loving father and in *Ezekiel* 16 of the robe woven for his lovely (if wanton) daughter Jerusalem by the doting Lord, 1 *Peter* 4:10 speaks of the varied gifts of Christians put to the service of God's manifold and interwoven designs—his *poikilos* grace. *Poikilos* means colourful; the intermingling of colours denotes also a richly embroidered, cleverly woven material.

A multi-faceted mystery

To gild the lily, as we have seen, the author of *Ephesians*, finding even this term inadequate to speak of the mystery of Christ in its reference to all Christians, Jew and Gentile, and the whole universe, employed his own. For him the mystery designed by the Creator of all things and now revealed through the Church is a *polypoikilos* wisdom, a *multi*coloured plan, a *many*-faceted reality, 'an eternal purpose realised in Christ Jesus our Lord' (3:10–11) and particularly through Jesus' Paschal Mystery. The word occurs nowhere else in the Bible, though we have seen Paul at pains to tease out the various dimensions of the mystery.

So it is not surprising if we find biblical and patristic writers having recourse to a range of terms and concepts to deal with the richness of this many-faceted mystery, the Church. Vatican II, in trying to come to grips with the mystery of the Church in this century, referred to the 'various images drawn from pastoral life, agriculture, building construction, and even from family and married life... in the writings of the biblical authors', listing the sheepfold, the flock, the tract of land, the vine, the building, the temple, the bride.[1] A few years previously Paul Minear had listed as many as 96 images of the Church in the New Testament, including beyond those major ones 32 'minor images', such as salt of the earth, a letter from Christ, fish net, boat, ark, elect lady.[2] Minear himself concentrates on those notions of the People of God, the New Creation, the Fellowship in Faith, the Body of Christ.

The Fathers, of course, particularly those with a relish for typology, found in the Scriptures abundant figurative material for discoursing on the Church, from Eve to Mary Magdalen, from Noah's ark to the sheet let down from heaven (in Peter's vision in *Acts* 10) containing all kinds of animals and reptiles and birds of the air (developed by Caesarius of Arles).[3] They could, we submit, with as much justification have adduced Joseph's 'technicolour dreamcoat' and the Lord's gift of a finely woven robe for his daughter Jerusalem.

Theologians today, in the wake of *Lumen Gentium*, are not averse to this abundance of images, if carrying scriptural support. An Orthodox commentator on the Constitution, Archbishop Basil Krivocheine, saw that the mystery requires this: 'An Orthodox Christian is sincerely glad that the text speaks not of the "nature" of the Church, as the first draft did, but of its "mystery". This mystery, inexpressible in concepts, reveals itself in the images of the Church that we find in the Old and New Testaments: sheepfold, field, vineyard...'[4] Pope John Paul II too, in situating lay people within the mystery of the Church in the wake of the 1987 Synod, has repeated recourse to the vineyard figure.[5]

For the Church—even more so the mystery of Christ in

all its dimensions—is a many-faceted reality. The limitation, the need to have recourse to figure, is on our side: we have difficulty, as biblical composers and Fathers did, grasping the reality in its entirety—not, however (we hasten to repeat as we have done from the outset of this book), because the Church as mystery is obscure; that would be to do a serious injustice to the sense of 'mystery'. Our difficulty comes from the magnitude, not the unintelligibility, of the divine plan for all people; Paul the Jew had difficulty with that plan, 'hidden for ages but now revealed', so we can expect a like challenge. The great number of writings on the Church over the ages testify to this response to the challenge. The Fathers, even from the apophatic East, in trying one image after another were not regarding the mystery as a puzzle, beyond our comprehension; for them, as De Lubac says in *Exégèse Médiévale*, 'omnia in figura':[6] everything is approached through figure and image. Modern commentators, like Avery Dulles, who suggest that images proliferate because the Church is a mystery and therefore 'not fully intelligible to the finite mind of man',[7] demonstrate an inadequate sense of mystery, as we have shown; better the phrase 'inexhaustible intelligibility', in another theologian's explanation of mystery.[8]

So, with our different concerns and perceptions, we are going to approach the many-faceted mystery of the Church now from one angle, now from another, like a jeweller studying the different facets of a diamond. In the process, different figures or images will appeal to us or require attention if we are to move towards grasping all that the Church is. Theologians have for some decades been endeavouring to sift through images of theological realities with a view to greater precision. Max Black[9] and Ian Ramsey began speaking of some images as models, on the analogy of scientific models: for Ramsey these 'form a collection of distinctive, reliable and easily specifiable techniques for talking about a reality which is ultimately mysterious',[10] and so preference should be given to 'disclosure models', yielding insight and understanding, rather than merely 'picture models'. For Sallie McFague in

Models of God[11], 'a model is a metaphor with "staying power". A model is a metaphor that has gained sufficient stability and scope so as to present a pattern for relatively comprehensive and coherent explanation.' Bernard Lonergan sees models as a help to method in theology generally;[12] John McIntyre[13] and John O'Grady[14] find models for Christology, and study of the Church has benefited likewise.

In his *Models of the Church* (1974) Dulles developed Minear's survey of biblical images in this direction; he speaks variously of approaches, types, models, aspects, dimensions, analogies, mind-sets. Rightly he places himself with his myriad predecessors in ecclesiology in claiming, 'I am seeking certain avenues of approach to the mystery of the Church';[15] Paul attempted no less. He distinguishes images and models: images 'employed reflectively and critically to deepen one's theoretical understanding of a reality' are models, whereas some models (institution, society, community) 'are not readily imaginable'.[16] Dulles says of his models what biblical, patristic, medieval and contemporary theologians could say of their figurative approaches: 'Each of the models calls attention to certain aspects of the Church that are less clearly brought out by the other models'.[17] It is, after all, a multicoloured reality, this mystery of the Church; the diamond needs viewing from one angle and another if we are to appreciate its richness.

Paradigm shifts

What is the most appropriate figure, image, model for this time or for that, it is difficult to say. Choice for emphasis will depend on a range of factors. Paul's development of the body of Christ as a figure of the Church was influenced by the culture he was exposed to. Typological Alexandria in patristic times felt freer in this field than more pedestrian Antioch. Bellarmine in post-Reformation times could see the Church in societal terms, a less biblical model for less biblical churchmen. Vatican II was emboldened to move beyond the approach of Pius XII's *Mystici Corporis Christi* of 1943,[18] selecting the People of God as a more suitable biblical figure. The 1985 Synod of Bishops revoked this preference, merely rehearsing the customary list of figures in favour of a description of the Church as 'the Mystery of Christ or the Church in Christ', and saying pointedly, 'We cannot replace a false unilateral vision of the Church as merely hierarchical with a new sociological conception which is also unilateral'.[19] The 1987 Synod on the laity, we have seen, highlighted the figure of the vineyard in particular.

We are at liberty to turn the diamond this way and that, appreciating the light from different facets as we do so; it is a diamond, after all, not one-dimensional glass. We expect changing emphasis in ecclesiology. Dulles, who observes that 'from 1600 to 1940 the juridical or societal model was in peaceful possession in the Catholic community',[20] further reinforces the need for development with his own later insights. In a 1982 study he reviewed 'the postconciliar crisis' in ecclesiology and came down in favour of a new model, the Church as community of disciples.[21] His adjustment in stance, and paradigm shifts generally, are legitimate.

The models and the mystery

This is not tantamount to saying that proper ecclesiology merely requires or merely aspires to a listing of all possible figures and models of Church, any one of which may happen to suit the mood and needs of the time. It is not sufficient merely to list them and compare them on the basis of strengths and weaknesses, as some ecclesiologists tend to do, and lamely admit that there is no one really adequate way of approaching Church, in this age or any other. O'-Grady speaks of 'a crisis of images' among Christians today, especially in regard to the Church: displacement of one image with a 'better' unsettles the faithful.[22] Though it may be strictly correct to say that 'we cannot integrate [the models of Church] into a single synthetic vision',[23] it is reprehensible to fail to recognise the adequacy of mystery as *the* matrix for comprehending and presenting Church, and to treat it as just one more (inadequate) model; without the diamond, remember, there are no facets. At the same time, we should heed De Lubac's reminder: 'No simple image or concept of the Church wholly succeeds in defining her, and the multiplicity of images and concepts offered by Scripture need simultaneous and inclusive treatment, and have been traditionally so treated.'[24]

For we are dealing pre-eminently with a mystery, the mystery of Christ, when we are contemplating Church; that has been the burden of this book. In this age or any other the Church should be seen for what it is, a mystery—properly understood, no matter which figure or another, biblical or patristic, it suits us to invoke for partial appreciation and presentation. It is a mystery of life, shared life, and so we can empathise to some extent with Tillard's proclamation, 'I strongly believe that *koinonia* is the basic definition of the Church',[25] even if we need to add that this sharing of life occurs within an eternal divine plan that is the mystery of Christ, and can perhaps be said to extend beyond the Church. It is a mystery within which the values that Jesus preached will be, and hopefully are being, realised among human beings and throughout the universe, and God's cause, the *basileia*, brought to completion. In the context of this mystery we can see in harmony our place in the Church and our life in the world.

Points for discussion

1. The word 'mystery' in theology has been often misinterpreted; those who have understood it better have called it something 'bright and dazzling' (Greeley) or 'startling yet simple' (Chesterton). How does theological writing that you know on the mystery of the Church bring out its marvellous variety or 'inexhaustible intelligibility' (O'Grady)? (Look, for instance, at #6 of *Lumen Gentium*.)
2. Theologians have developed models in theology; Avery Dulles' *Models of the Church* is well-known. Which

model of Church appeals to you the most? Can you appreciate that your parents may have been brought up to a different model of Church in practice? Do you see that the mystery of the Church is tolerant of a range of models?

3. Why is it important that we have a sound model of the Church to live by? Show how our model of Church affects sacramental life, Church organisation, catechesis, social sensitivity, etc.
4. Can you discern different models of Church operating in other Christian communities (evangelical churches, for example)? What do we as Catholics stand to learn from this? Relate the variety of models to the mystery of the Church.

6
LIVING THE MYSTERY OF LIFE

In *The Innocence of Father Brown* G. K. Chesterton, that lover of paradox, has his priestly detective make one of his typical distinctions: 'The modern mind always mixes up two different ideas: mystery in the sense of what is marvellous, and mystery in the sense of what is complicated.' It is a clarification that would throw light on much writing on the Church, as we have tried to show in this book. What is marvellous need not be complicated or obscure; Father Brown applies this truth to a miracle, but it is equally applicable to the mystery of the Church, which like a miracle is 'startling yet simple'. It is to be hoped these chapters on the Church, meant neither for the specialist nor for the beginner, have not proved to be complicated and thus obscure the marvel.

Because, if the Church is a mystery of life and is envisaged most adequately that way, then that life is for living, not for merely pondering or debating. If it is important to bring our thinking on Church into touch with Scriptures and Fathers, to see its relation to *basileia* and *koinonia*, that marvellous share in divine life, it is equally important to show that the mystery of life can be lived. We have not paused at every stage of this work to tease out those vital implications, though the discussion pointers after each chapter were intended to promote such reflection. So it is time now to place the accent more on living; accepting the Church as mystery means a particular direction to our thinking that should affect our living.

Living the mystery

That is easily said, accepting the Church as mystery; an

ingrained notion of mystery as puzzle makes it difficult for us to see mystery as Paul would have us see it, God's great design for all he has created. Once, however, we crash that barrier and redirect that habit, several advantages flow from our fresh understanding of Church. By adopting Paul's understanding we discard the pious agnosticism that views the truths and realities of faith as obscure 'mysteries' and that retreats in particular from the mystery of Church. We still find this vast sacred reality, this mystery, 'bright and dazzling' (with Greeley) and 'marvellous' (with Father Brown); but it does not deprive us of a recognition of God's ways as he conducts this design for our benefit, nor does it discourage our entry into contemporary issues affecting the Church. That is a bonus from continuing Catholic emphasis on tradition—that there are paths, ways of entering and re-entering the community's experience of God's action: biblical ways, liturgical ways, doctrinal ways, catechetical ways. Hence the emphasis in this book on Bible and Fathers and other magisterial statement on the mystery of the Church. The mystery, in other words, revealed though it is, does not defy our understanding.

Secondly, by accepting the Church as mystery, we enjoy an expanded perspective that allows for no false opposition in our lives between Church and world. The mystery of Christ that includes the Church under its ecclesial dimension includes also the rest of God's creation under other dimensions. As Vatican II's *Gaudium et Spes* insisted, there is no real antithesis between Christians' membership of Church and their worldly, social, professional involvement; these come together 'in one vital synthesis' in the context of God's plan. As people of this world, just as Jesus was of this world, we are also members of the community of Jesus' disciples, the Church; understanding the mystery of Christ allows us to accept this further truth. There is more to be said of this in a moment.

Again, seeing the Church as mystery, a concept more basic than any model or figure of Church, be it institution or body or society, allows us to get beyond irritations and vexations that come to us from living in that community. In particular, perhaps, it gives us the vision to look beyond, if not quite overlook, the behaviour towards us of churchmen and churchwomen who may not have realised yet in their own lives the values of the *basileia* that Jesus set as a goal for his community. Too many people carry as a burden through life a history of ill-feeling against Church leaders at various levels that can make them feel estranged from the Church and even leads many to sever connections with the institution. Yet the mystery, the vast sacred design by which 'he has chosen us in Christ before the foundation of the world', brings out the true pettiness of these vexations and correspondingly dignifies our participation in the divine offer of life which Church represents. We need at times to be able to fall back to that wider perspective.

In doing this we are in our daily lives invoking a more adequate theology of Church; for we are all theologians, and it is the Church in particular that prompts that theologising process by which we try to make sense of what we believe. To the professional theologians in the community this book suggests that an understanding of Church as mystery enables them to develop a truly adequate theology of Church, one that is not partial or skewed; chapter one indicated that such adequacy in ecclesiology is not generally found and that the drift of *Lumen Gentium* has not everywhere been respected. Behind the models and figures and images of Church lies the manifold (*polypoikilos*) mystery that accommodates them all; without the diamond there are no facets, we suggested. A theology of Church as mystery allows for a balanced extrapolation of a theology of ministry, for example, a theology of collegiality, a theology of lay participation, a theology of Christianity's role in the market place.

In particular, Catholic churchmen and theologians (like Yves Congar) viewing the Church as mystery—on the model of Paul—are thus provided with a basis for establishing and promoting relations with Eastern Christians and other Western Christians from whom we have for too long been divided. The divine plan, the mystery of Christ to which Paul was granted insight,envisaged not division between Christians, not even between Jew and Gentile, but a union ensured by the breaking down of the wall and bringing hostility to an end (*Eph* 2:14–16). Small wonder that in our day a proper understanding of the total mystery provides a basis for the Christian community's relation with Judaism, and that truly universal theologians like Raimundo Panikkar find in it also grounds for relationship with Hinduism and other world religions.

What a theology of Church as mystery gives us, in short, is breadth of perspective, widening of horizons. On our part this involves ideally a sufficient and continuing education in faith: familiarity with the Bible (particularly the Wisdom books of the Old Testament and Paul in the New), some schooling in theology, savouring those great agents of tradition, the Fathers, like Origen and Justin, Irenaeus and Augustine (neglected today even in seminary programs). We need as well to tap into the approach of Eastern and other Western traditions of Church and other Christian mysteries. An impossible ideal? For many people, perhaps, but happily there are today those working to open up these treasures of Christian tradition, this 'spring of living waters', in the words of John Paul II, to the greater numbers coming to drink. For these fortunate drinkers the Church can appear as 'a great mystery and wonderful sacrament', as De Lubac reminds us the Roman liturgy already presented her. Seeing the Church also as sacrament, as Augustine did and Vatican II again does, can soften our approach to her institutional aspects, while reinforcing her incarnational and visible character (in case 'mystery' is too spooky a notion) and promoting our sensitivity to our responsibilities of witness and mission.

A life to be lived

The Church, of course, is not primarily an institution. It is not primarily an experience of ritual and worship. It is not even a belief system, different from other belief systems and approaches to reality. The Church comes to us as an offer of life, as Jesus did: 'I have come that they may have life, and have it to the full' (*Jn* 10:10). That is why Church leaders at Vatican II and the 1985 Synod that looked back on it promoted a theology of church as communion, sharing, *koinonia*. It is life that is on offer and that we accept by joining the community. Concern about institutional features of Church, about the quality of liturgy and its rituals, about contemporary Church teachings should not obscure that accent on life, life to the fullest. 'I set before you this day life and death', said the God of the Old Testament to his people; 'choose life' (*Dt* 30:15,19). In the Church we have that offer of life embodied and perpetuated. What a pity if we do not perceive that this is what Church is for us.

All this presumes that our local church is a community that is characterised by sharing, fellowship, participation, and is not an impassive, private, uncaring congregation showing little sign of vitality. The New Testament statement of *koinonia* reflects a community conscious of the gift of life from God in Jesus and ready to extend that gift to others, especially those in need. Such a theology of Church is providential at a time when larger institutions are failing, numbers declining, clergy and religious dwindling, and when correspondingly smaller groups within the community are arising to minister life to one another. We have emerged from a less interactive institution into a community where we are invited to participate and share—in a mystery of life. Is that your experience of Church?

This understanding of Church is also the best basis for regarding the churches within the Church, as Polycarp and Irenaeus, Cyprian and Augustine in their day recognised and the Anglican-Roman Catholic International Commission (ARCIC) acknowledges in ours. Pope and bishop could differ on matters (to them important, if less so to us these days) and yet agree 'to share communion with one another'. In our day we have seen pope and patriarch embracing each other, regretting differences and recriminations between 'sister churches' of East and West, if not yet sure of the precise way ahead. Irenaeus' dictum in the second century sets the principle: 'The difference in the fast confirms the agreement in the faith'. There is every reason to build communion on that basis, not to rupture it by ex-communication. Before that dictum mere shibboleths, verbal niceties, pale in importance; faith is the canon. Happily we are seeing dialogue between the Roman Catholic community and the Anglican, Protestant, Orthodox communities, and at a local level interchurch sharing of various kinds.

The Church is a communion, after all. Again semantics gets in the way, as with 'mystery'. We Catholics tend with communion to think of 'Holy Communion', a rite that is a holy and perhaps very private moment for us. Yet the word should suggest sharing and communication, a sensitivity to others. The New Testament and the Fathers taught us to think of communion in both ways, a sharing in the body and blood of Jesus and sharing with those less fortunate. The World Council of Churches puts it well: 'As participants in the Eucharist we prove inconsistent if we are not actively participating in this ongoing restoration of the world's situation and the human condition.' Life is a gift to be shared.

Life in the world

So the Eucharist should send us out into the world to bring life to it. Is there no limit to our sharing what we enjoy in the mystery of the Church? Certainly we can read the Scriptures, at least the bulk of them, and gain no impression that the world lies within the mystery of Christ, let alone the Church; life is for people, *our* people. So we are predisposed to see the world, if not as hostile, at least as irrelevant to the sharing of life that occurs within the Church. Pastors down the ages have warned of involvement in the world, religious life has held up as an ideal *separatio mundi*, separation from the world. Jesus himself would not pray for the world (*Jn* 17:9). The New Testament and then Augustine encouraged us to see life in this city as temporary, evanescent, and to seek life in one that is to come, the city of God. Magisterial statement, if distinguishing the secular from the religious, tended to inveigh against secularism, with little positive to be said for a necessary process of secularisation. No, life did not lie in the world—despite all the time we spent there and despite all the guidance we needed for our necessary involvement there.

But the truth about God's world, about the true dimensions of the mystery of Christ, had to emerge despite the predisposition against it—a predisposition going back to dualistic attitudes to spirit and matter well before Christianity. The Bible as a whole does in fact give us the total picture of the mystery of Christ; the world does have a place in God's plan, Paul reminded us with the encouragement of Old Testament sages. The human spirit, too, came to a realisation (even without heeding *Genesis* 1) that our responsibility extends to the universe as a whole; conservation lobby groups made us aware of this, and a creation theology supplied a theoretical framework. At least the laity in the Church intuitively acknowledged that the world is the arena where the community of the Church lives up to the values of the *basileia* that Jesus, who hardly ever mentioned the word Church, was forever holding up as the ideal for his disciples. The Eucharist sends us out into the world to share life there.

And the world needs us as missionaries of life—the world in the sense of the people in it (the *kosmos* for whom John's Jesus would not pray, and yet whom God so loved as to send his only son to give it life: *Jn* 3:16) or its structures and attitudes and inequalities. If God accepted the world in creating it, and if Jesus accepted it in his incarnation, he is also quick to tell us at the very outset of his ministry (in Mark) that the arrival of the *basileia* in him means repentance and conversion, and (in Luke) that he has come to right all those inequalities. So the true attitude of Church to world is one of acceptance, not that erstwhile grudging acceptance but yet a liberating acceptance; the world needs transforming, enlivening. We the

Church are the ones to do it.

In the overall design that is the mystery of Christ, then, the Church is really not in opposition to the world but, as Johannes Metz says, guarantees its true, liberated worldliness in a way nothing else can: 'The Church exists for the sake of the world.' Like Jesus, the Church brings life to the world. Daily we bring it life by living out the values of the *basileia* there; the world needs us to exemplify the Beatitudes in its midst. In Moltmann's phrase, we are like 'an arrow sent out into the world to point to the future', but also to redeem the present. This mighty enterprise, this vast design that God has for Church and world, is truly marvellous, a mystery, 'bright and dazzling'. No wonder that theologians over the ages have had recourse to one generally inadequate figure or model after another. While profiting from them all, let us stay with mystery, the mystery of life that the Church is.

ENDNOTES

Introduction

1. Henri De Lubac, *The Splendour of the Church* (2nd ed.) Paulist, Glen Rock, 1963, p. 17.
2. Pope Pius XII, *Divino Afflante Spiritu*, Vatican, Rome, 1943.
3. id., *Mystici Corporis Christi*, Vatican, Rome, 1943.
4. id., *Mediator Dei*, Vatican, Rome, 1947.
5. *Humani Generis*, Vatican, Rome, 1950.
6. Vatican II, *Lumen Gentium*, Vatican, Rome, 1964.
7. Pope Paul VI, *Ecclesiam Suam*, Vatican, Rome, 1964.
8. Extraordinary Synod of Bishops, *Final Report*, Vatican, Rome, 1985.
9. Pope John Paul II, *Christifideles Laici*, Vatican, Rome, 1989. For a full commentary on the ecclesiology of this half century, see A. Dulles, 'A half century of ecclesiology', *Theological Studies* 50, (1989), pp. 419–442.
10. Augustine, *De Unitate Ecclesiae*, I, 20, 56 (*Patrologia Latina*, 43, 434).

Chapter 1

1. 'Flight into mystery', *Die Zeit*, December 6, 1985.
2. Extraordinary Synod of Bishops, *Final Report*, Vatican, Rome, 1985.
3. Ibid.
4. Extraordinary Synod of Bishops, *Message to the People of God*, Vatican, Rome, 1985, II.
5. ibid.
6. Pope Paul VI, *Ecclesiam Suam*, Vatican, Rome, 1964.
7. Matthias Scheeben, *The Mysteries of Christianity*, St Louis, London, Herder, 1946, p. 2.
8. Andrew Greeley, *The Great Mysteries: An Essential Catechism*, Seabury, New York, 1976, xvi–xvii. Cf. Edward Robinson, *The Language of Mystery*, London, SCM, 1987, for similar inadequacies.

9. Avery Dulles, *Models of the Church*, Doubleday, Garden City, 1974, pp. 15–16.
10. Dumitru Staniloae, 'The mystery of the Church', in *Church, Kingdom, World: The Church as Mystery and Prophetic Sign* (W.C.C. Faith and Order Papers No.130), ed. G. Limouris, World Council of Churches, Geneva, 1986, pp. 50, 52.
11. Yves Congar, *The Mystery of the Church*, London, Chapman, 1965.
12. H. Clerissac, *The Mystery of the Church*, Sheed and Ward, London, 1937.
13. R. F. Trevett, *The Church: Christ's Mystery and Sacrament*, Burns and Oates, London, 1961, p. 13.
14. John Powell, *The Mystery of the Church*, Bruce, Milwaukee, 1967, p. 13.
15. Vatican II, *Lumen Gentium*, Vatican, Rome, 1964, 2.
16. Ibid., 2.
17. Ibid., 5.
18. Ibid., 6.
19. William Barclay trans., *The New Testament: A New Translation, Collins Fontana, Glasgow, 1976.*
20. Pope John Paul II, *Christifideles Laici*, Vatican, Rome, 1989.
21. Raymond Brown, *The Semitic Background of the Term 'Mystery' in the New Testament*, Fortress, Philadelphia, 1968.
22. Gunther Bornkamm, '*mysterion*', in *Theological Dictionary of the New Testament* IV, ed. G. Kittel, Eerdmans, Grand Rapids, 1967.
23. Chrys Caragounis, *The Ephesian Mysterion* (Coniectanea Biblica NT Series 8), Gleerup, Lund, 1977, p. 134.
24. See Charles Hill, 'The mystery of Christ: clue to Paul's thinking on wisdom', *Heythrop Journal* 25, (1984), pp. 475–83. Cf. L. Bouyer, *Liturgical Piety*, University of Notre Dame Press, Notre Dame, 1955, pp. 93–98.
25. Interpretation depends on manuscript readings, especially at 1 *Cor* 2:1 and *Col* 2:2. (The plural of *mysterion* has a different sense, and is not considered

here.)
26. *The Shepherd of Hermas*, *Vision*, 2, 4, 1 (*Sources Chrétiennes* 53, 96).
27. Origen, *Commentary on the Song of Songs* (*Patrologia Graeca* 13, 134).
28. Augustine, *Commentary on Ps CXXVIII* (*Corpus Christianorum Latinorum* 40, 1882). See E. G. Hinson (ed.), *Understandings of the Church*, Fortress, Philadelphia, 1986, for further patristic statements on the Church.
29. Henri De Lubac, *The Splendour of the Church* (2nd ed.), Paulist, Glen Rock, 1963, p. 17.
30. Ibid., p. 19.
31. Ibid., p. 28.
32. Ibid., p. 37.
33. Ibid., p. 33.
34. Ibid., p. 39.
35. Ibid., p. 71.
36. Ibid., p. 125.
37. Extraordinary Synod of Bishops, *Message to the People of God*, II.
38. id., *Final Report*, II A1.
39. Vatican II, *Gaudium et Spes*, Vatican, Rome, 1964.
40. Cf. H. Pottmeyer, 'The Church as mysterium and as Institution', *Concilium*, 188, 6 (1986), pp. 99–109.
41. Cardinal Ratzinger, *L'Osservatore Romano*, 26 Nov. 1985.
42. Cf. Vatican II, *Lumen Gentium*, 8.
43. *Final Report*, II A3.
44. Extraordinary Synod of Bishops, *Message* III.
45. Pope John Paul II, *Christifideles Laici*, Vatican, Rome, 1989, 8, 9, 18, 19, ...
46. Vatican II, *Lumen Gentium*, 1.
47. Augustine, *Epistulae*, 138,1,7, (*Patrologia Latina* 33, 527).
48. id., *Contra Faustum Manichaeum* 19, 11 (*Patrologia Latina* 42, 355).
49. De Lubac, op. cit., p. 31.
50. Congar, *Cette Eglise que J'Aime* (This Church that I Love), Du Cerf, Paris, 1968, p. 52.

51. Ibid., p. 56.
52. Vatican II, *Lumen Gentium*, 8.
53. Quoted by G. Gassmann in 'The Church as sacrament, sign, and instrument: The reception of this ecclesiological understanding in ecumenical debate', in *Church, Kingdom, World: The Church as Mystery and Prophetic Sign*, p. 4.
54. Congar, *Diversity and Communion*, Twenty-Third Publications, Mystic, 1985, p. 21.
55. D. Coffey, 'The Church as Community', *Faith and Culture* (1990) 44–55.

Chapter 2

1. Jerome Hamer, *The Church is a Communion*, Chapman, London, 1964.
2. The text of Cardinal Hume's address appeared in *The Tablet*, 7 Dec. 1985, p. 1297.
3. Extraordinary Synod of Bishops, *Final Report*, Vatican, Rome, 1985.
4. William Barclay, trans., *The New Testament: A New Translation*, Collins Fontana, Glasgow, 1976.
5. Anglican Roman Catholic International Commission, *Final Report* CTS/SPCK, London, 1982, 4.
6. *The Tablet*, p. 1297.
7. Ernst Käsemann, 'Unity and multiplicity in the New Testament doctrine of Church', in *New Testament Questions of Today*, SCM, London, 1969, pp. 252–59. Cf. Congar, *Diversity and Communion*, pp. 9–14.
8. George Panikulam, *Koinonia in the New Testament* (Analecta Biblica 85), Biblical Institute Press, Rome, 1979, p. 129. Cf. Pier Cesare Bovi, *Koinonia, L'Idea della Communione nell' Ecclesiologia Recente e nel Nuovo Testamento*, Paideia, Brescia, 1977, for a less thorough review of NT data and more comprehensive survey of theological writing.
9. Panikulam, p. 5.
10. Extraordinary Synod of Bishops, *Final Report*, C1.
11. Cf. J–M. Tillard, '*Final Report* of the last Synod', *Concilium*, 188, 6 (1986), p. 66.

12. Pope John Paul II, *Christifideles Laici*, Vatican, Rome, 1989.
13. Anglican Roman Catholic International Commission, op. cit., Introduction 5.
14. World Council of Churches, *Baptism, Eucharist and Ministry* (Faith and Order Paper 111), World Council of Churches, Geneva, 1982.
15. Dumitru Staniloae, 'The mystery of the Church' in *Church, Kingdom, World. The Church as Mystery and Prophetic Sign* (W.C.C. Faith and Order Papers No. 130), ed. G. Limouris, World Council of Churches, Geneva, 1986, pp. 52–53.
16. Augustine, *De Unitate Ecclesiae*, I, 20, 56 (*Patrologia Latina* 43, 434). Cf. Brunner, 'The Church is nothing other than men [sic] in fellowship with God and in fellowship with each other'. (*Dogmatics* 3), Lutterworth, London, 1962, p. 21.
17. Henri De Lubac, *The Splendour of the Church* (2nd ed.), Paulist, Glen Rock, 1963, p. 17.
18. Hamer, op. cit., pp. 163–64.
19. Anglican Roman Catholic International Commission, op. cit., p. 52, 'Authority in the Church I', 1.
20. Avery Dulles, *Models of the Church*, Doubleday, Garden City, 1974, p. 55. Dulles has had something of a rethink of this matter in *A Church to Believe In*, Crossroad, New York, 1982, pp. 1–18.
21. Cyprian, quoted in Yves Congar, *Diversity and Communion*, Twenty Third Publications, Mystic, p. 24.
22. Augustine, *De Baptismo* III, 3,5 (*Patrologia Latina* 43, 141).
23. De Lubac, op. cit., p. 35.
24. J. Gaden, 'The Church and Churches of the Apostles', *Colloquium* 19 (May 1987), p. 19.
25. Anglican Roman Catholic International Commission, op. cit., Introduction 7.
26. Panikulam, op. cit., p. 107.
27. World Council of Churches, op. cit., p. 2.
28. John Damascene, *On Orthodox Faith* 4 (*Patrologia Graeca* 94,1153).

29. World Council of Churches, op. cit., p. 14.
30. Justin, *Apology*, 1, 6, 7.
31. Anglican Roman Catholic International Commission, op. cit., Introduction 8.
32. Augustine, *Contra Cresconium* III, 35, 39 (*Patrologia Latina* 43, 517).
33. Vatican II, *Lumen Gentium*, 23 and note 107.
34. Anglican Roman Catholic International Commission, op. cit., p. 55, 'Authority in the Church I', 8.
35. Pope Paul VI, quoted in Congar, op. cit., p. 88.
36. *The Tablet*, p. 1297.
37. Augustine, *Epistulae* 54, 2, 2, (*Patrologia Latina* 33,200).
38. Irenaeus, quoted in Eusebius, *Historia Ecclesiastica* 5, 24 (italics in quotation added).
39. Congar, op. cit.
40. Barclay trans., op. cit.
41. Clement of Alexandria, *Paedagogus* I, 6 (*Patrologia Graeca* 8, 281).
42. Staniloae, op. cit., pp. 51–52.

Chapter 3

1. Alfred Loisy, quoted in Hans Küng, *The Church*, Search Press, London, 1968, p. 43.
2. Ernst Käsemann, 'On the subjectof primitive Christian apocalyptic', in *New Testament Questions of Today*, SCM, London, 1969, p. 122.
3. Raymond Brown, *The Gospel According to John* I–XII (Anchor Bible 29), Doubleday, Garden City, 1966, cx.
4. id., *The Churches the Apostles Left Behind*, Paulist, New York, 1981, p. 51.
5. Vatican II, *Lumen Gentium* 5, Vatican, Rome, 1964.
6. Ibid., 3.
7. Vatican II, *Gaudium et Spes* 39, Vatican, Rome, 1964.
8. Extraordinary Synod of Bishops, *Final Report*, II A3.
9. Jürgen Moltmann, *The Church in the Power of the Spirit*, Harper and Row, New York, 1977, p. 196.
10. Küng, op. cit., pp. 92–93.

11. Jan Lochman, 'Church and world in the light of the Kingdom of God', in *Church, Kingdom, World. The Church as Mystery and Prophetic Sign* (World Council of Churches Faith and Order Papers, No. 130), ed. G. Limouris, W.C.C., Geneva, 1986, p. 70.
12. Staniloae, op. cit., p. 56.
13. See Avery Dulles, *Models of the Church*, Doubleday, Garden City, 1974, pp. 44–45 for these views: also his essay, 'Catholic ecclesiology since Vatican II', *Concilium* 188, 6 (1986), pp. 4–5.
14. See Charles Hill, 'Synoptic *basileia* and Pauline *mysterion*', *Estudios Biblicos* 45 (1987), pp. 309–24.
15. J. A. Fitzmyer, *The Gospel According to Luke* I–IX (Anchor Bible 28), Doubleday, Garden City, 1981, p. 707.
16. Origen, *Comm. in Matt*, tom xiv, 7 (*Patrologia Graeca* 13, 1197). Cf. Augustine a few centuries later: 'God's *mysterium* is none other than Christ' (Epistulae 187: PL 33, 845).
17. Tertullian, *Adversus Marcionem* IV, 33,8 (*Patrologia Graeca* 2,441).
18. W. L. Lane, *The Gospel According to Mark* (New International Commentary), Eerdmans, Grand Rapids, p. 58. Cf. J. Marcus, *The Mystery of the Kingdom of God*, Scholars' Press, Atlanta, 1986, pp. 44–47.
19. H. C. Kee, *Community of the New Age: Studies in Mark's Gospel*, Westminster, Philadelphia, 1977, p. 66.
20. Vincent Taylor, *The Gospel According to St Mark*, Macmillan, London, 1966, p. 255.
21. Ernst Käsemann, 'Blind alleys in the "Jesus of history" controversy', *New Testament Questions of Today*, op. cit., p. 62.
22. James Dunn, *Unity and Diversity in the New Testament*, SCM, London, 1977, p. 219.
23. Küng, op. cit., p.57.
24. Brown, *The Gospel According to John* I–XII, op. cit., p. 393.
25. Rudolf Bultmann, *The History of the Synoptic Tradition*, Blackwell, Oxford, 1968, p. 325, note 1.

26. Käsemann, op. cit., p. 128.
27. For details of Paul's use of *basileia*, see Charles Hill, 'Synoptic *basileia* and Pauline *mysterion*'.
28. Lochman, op. cit., p. 67.
29. Vatican II, *Lumen Gentium* 5, Vatican, Rome, 1964.

Chapter 4

1. See Charles Hill, 'The dimensions of salvation history in the Wisdom Books', *Scripture* 19, 1967, pp. 97–106.
2. William Barclay trans., *The New Testament. A New Translation*, Collins Fontana, Glasgow, 1976.
3. Johannes Metz, *Theology of the World*, Herder and Herder, New York, 1969, p. 35.
4. Henri De Lubac, *The Splendour of the Church* (2nd ed.), Paulist, Glen Rock, 1963, p. 93.
5. Vatican II, *Gaudium et Spes*, Vatican, Rome, 1964, 43.
6. Vatican II, op. cit., 44.
7. Extraordinary Synod of Bishops, *Final Report*, II A1.
8. Ibid., II D1–2. See J. M. Tillard, '*Final Report* of the last Synod', *Concilium* 188, 6 (1986), pp. 65–67.
9. Pope Paul VI, *Evangelii Nuntiandi*, Vatican, Rome, 1975.
10. Dietrich Bonhoeffer, *Letters and Papers from Prison*, Fontana, London, 1953, 108.
11. Ibid., p. 160.
12. Ibid., p. 91, entry of April 30, 1944.
13. Ibid., p. 95, entry of May 5, 1944.
14. Vatican II, *Decree on the Apostolate of the Laity*, Vatican, Rome, 1964, 7.
15. Vatican II, *Gaudium et Spes*, op. cit., 39–54.
16. Karl Rahner, 'Christology within an evolutionary view of the world', *Theological Investigations* V, DLT, London, 1966, p. 190.
17. Metz, op. cit., pp. 47–48.
18. Jan Lochman, 'Church and world in the light of the Kingdom of God', in *Church, Kingdom, World. The Church as Mystery and Prophetic Sign*, (World Council of Churches Faith and Order Papers No.130), ed. G.

Limouris, W.C.C., Geneva, 1986, p. 64.
19. Karl Rahner, quoted in Metz, op. cit., pp. 93–94.
20. Bonhoeffer, op. cit., p. 112.
21. Metz, op. cit., pp. 49–50.
22. Cf. Avery Dulles, *Models of the Church,* Doubleday, Garden City, 1974, Ch. 6, and Bonhoeffer, op. cit., p. 166.
23. Pope Paul VI, *Ecclesiam Suam*, ECTS translation of AAS 56, 1964, p. 641, where the Pope's '*homines*' has been rendered as 'world' (in keeping with the Johannine reference, it is true).
24. World Council of Churches, *Gathered for Life*, W.C.C., Geneva, 1983, p. 50.
25. Yves Congar, *Cette Eglise que J'Aime*, (This Church that I Love), du Cerf, Paris, 1968, p. 46. Metz, in *Theology of the World* p. 26, speaks of the hypostatic union between man, his world and the Eternal Word.
26. Congar, *Lay People in the Church*, Bloomsbury, London, 1957, p. 88.
27. 'The mystery of the Church and the Eucharist in the light of the mystery of Holy Trinity', *One in Christ*, 19 (1983), p. 188.
28. Jürgen Moltmann, *Theology of Hope*, SCM, London, 1967, p. 328.
29. Henri De Lubac, *The Splendour of the Church* (2nd ed.), Paulist, Glen Rock, 1963, p. 33. De Lubac cites *De Veritate*, no.29, a.4, obj.5.
30. Metz, op. cit., p. 50, note 51.
31. Augustine, *Sermo XCVI*, 8 (*Patrologia Latina* 38, 588).
32. Thomas Aquinas, *Summa Theologiae*, 1a, q.1, a.3, ad 2.

Chapter 5

1. Vatican II, *Lumen Gentium* 6, Vatican, Rome, 1964.
2. Paul Minear, *Images of the Church in the New Testament*, Westminster, Philadelphia, 1960.
3. Cf. Yves Congar, *L'Eglise de Saint Augstin à l'Epoque Moderne*, du Cerf, Paris, 1970.

4. Basil Krivocheine, 'La Constitution dogmatique De Ecclesia: Point de vue d'un Orthodoxe', *Irenikon*, 39, (1966) p. 478.
5. Pope John Paul II, *Christifideles Laici*, Vatican, Rome, 1987.
6. Henri De Lubac, *Exégèse Médiéval*, II–II, Aubier, Paris, 1964, p. 62. A less happy reference to St John Chrysostom, who, as Antiochene, was in fact less prone to typological interpretation than the Alexandrians.
7. Avery Dulles, *Models of the Church*, Doubleday, Garden City, 1974, p. 15.
8. John O'Grady, *Models of Jesus*, Image Books, Garden City, 1981, p. 22.
9. Max Black, *Models and Metaphors*, Cornell University Press, Ithaca, 1962.
10. Ian Ramsey, *Models and Mystery*, OUP, New York, 1964, p. 4.
11. Sallie McFague, *Models of God*, SCM, London, 1987, p. 34.
12. Bernard Lonergan, *Method in Theology*, DLT, London, 1973, xii: 'By a model is not meant something to be copied or imitated. By a model is not meant a description of reality or a hypothesis about reality. It is simply an intelligible, interlocking set of terms and relations that it may be well to have about when it comes to describing reality or to forming hypotheses. As the proverb, so the model is something worth keeping in mind when one confronts a situation or tackles a job.'
13. John McIntyre, *The Shape of Christology*, SCM, London, 1966.
14. O'Grady, op. cit.
15. Dulles, op. cit., p. 9.
16. Ibid., p. 21.
17. Ibid., p. 7.
18. Pope Pius XII, *Mystici Corporis Christi*, Vatican, Rome, 1943.
19. Extraordinary Synod of Bishops, *Final Report* II A3,

Vatican, Rome, 1985.
20. Dulles, op. cit., p. 28.
21. id., *A Church to Believe In*, Crossroad, New York, 1982, pp. 6–7. Cf. Dulles' 'Catholic ecclesiology since Vatican II', *Concilium*, 188, 6, 1986, pp. 3–13.
22. O'Grady, op. cit., p. 27.
23. Dulles, op. cit., p. 8.
24. De Lubac, *The Church: Paradox and Mystery*, Ecclesia Press, Shannon, 1969, p. 23.
25. J–M. Tillard, 'Koinonia: Sacrament', *One in Christ*, 22, (1986), p. 114.

GLOSSARY

APOCALYPTIC literature (in the Bible, for instance) endeavours to provide special access to revelation (Grk *apocalypsis*) through a series of visions, dreams, exotic imagery dealing especially with the world's end.

The APOPHATIC tradition in theology stresses what cannot be known (about God, e.g.), thus proceeding rather by way of elimination of negatives than by demonstration of positives.

ARCIC (Anglican-Roman Catholic International Commission), established in 1966 by Pope Paul VI and Archbishop Michael Ramsey of Canterbury, produced a series of joint statements collected in *The Final Report* (1981). ARCIC II has continued to meet.

BASILEIA is the word that appears on Jesus' lips in the Greek New Testament (usually, but often unhappily, translated 'kingdom') for God's reign and value system that he comes to inaugurate.

CANON, a Greek word for yardstick or norm (cf. Canon Law), is applied to that group of scriptural works found normative for a particular community, e.g. Jews, Orthodox, Catholics, Protestants.

CHRISTOLOGY is the branch of theology that studies the life, ministry, person and significance of Jesus as well as the broader dimensions of the mystery of Christ.

COMMUNION is from the Latin for sharing, fellowship, participation (Grk *koinonia*). It is used in a particular sense for sharing in the body and blood of the Lord.

COSMOS, a Greek word for the whole universe, is also used in the New Testament for this world and/or the people in it. Philosophers devise a COSMOLOGY to account for the makeup of the universe.

DEMYTHOLOGISING is the process of distinguishing the

myth, or figurative overlay, that in the course of time or literary composition has been applied to a person or event highlighting its significance.

DOMINICAL, an adjective from Lat. *dominus*, 'lord', is applied to sayings of the Lord Jesus in the New Testament to distinguish them from others.

DUALISM, from Lat. *duo*, 'two', is a philosophical approach that tends to separate and even oppose what should rather be integrated, e.g. spirit and matter, soul and body.

ECCLESIA is a Greek (and then Latin) word for Church. ECCLESIOLOGY studies the Church or ECCLESIAL matters.

ECUMENICAL, an adjective from Grk *oikoumeme*, 'the inhabited (lit. 'housed') part of the world' (Grk *oikos*, 'house'), has the meaning universal (when applied to Church Councils) or embracing all religious groups and not simply one's own.

ESCHATOLOGICAL, an adjective from Grk *eschaton*, 'last thing, end, goal', has the sense of looking towards or moving to the goal instead of remaining static.

EVANGELII NUNTIANDI, Pope Paul VI's apostolic exhortation following the 1974 Synod of Bishops on evangelisation in the modern world.

EXEGESIS is the Greek term for explanation, applied especially to the Scriptures, a process in which the EXEGETE brings linguistic, historical and literary skills to bear on the text.

FATHERS (of the Church) were the great spokesmen and teachers in the first eight centuries of Christianity, East and West, whose theological works are extant. Few women's works have been preserved.

GAUDIUM ET SPES, lit. 'Joy and Hope', is the title of Vatican II's Constitution on the Church in the modern world, which is thus optimistic in tone.

HYPOSTASIS is a Greek word which can mean person; so we speak of the HYPOSTATIC union by which in the person of Jesus, divine and human natures are united. HYPOSTATISATION (e.g. of the figure of Wisdom in biblical works) would therefore be more than personification, a mere figure of speech.

IMMANENCE, from the Latin for remaining within, is one of the divine attributes by which God is present within his world and not simply superior to it. Denying the latter and emphasising only the former is known as IMMANENTISM.

INCARNATIONAL theology stresses God's sacramental way of dealing with us so that spiritual goods come to us through tangible realities (Jesus, the Church, the Bible, the Eucharist, daily events, etc.).

JOHANNINE, the adjective from John, is applied to the New Testament works bearing that name.

KINGDOM, the usual (if inadequate) translation of *basileia* in the New Testament, is there less a geographical or political entity than the reign of God and his will and values that Jesus comes to inaugurate, in keeping with the Old Testament's picture of Yahweh as king.

KOINONIA, Greek for sharing, fellowship, participation, communion. The New Testament uses it of God's sharing life with us, and our sharing with others.

LUMEN GENTIUM (Lat. for 'light of the nations') is the title of Vatican II's Constitution on the Church, where Jesus and by implication the Church are said to attract all peoples (a phrase used by the prophet Second Isaiah [42.6] of the Suffering Servant).

MAGISTERIUM, Lat. for the office of teacher (*magister*), is applied to those who teach by right of office in the Church, especially (but not exclusively) pope and bishops.

MINISTRY, from the Latin for service (Grk *diakonia*), is spoken of in the New Testament in reference to Jesus' life and the contribution of Christians in the areas of faith, life and worship as a result of gifts given to them for the benefit of the community. In the course of time some MINISTERS were ordained and vested with authority.

A MODEL in theology, as in other sciences, is an image or analogy that has the capacity to assist in explanation of the whole reality (such as the servant model of Church).

MODERNISM is a term applied to the teaching of some Catholic scholars a century ago who wanted the Church to come to terms with scientific, critical and historical developments in the world following the Enlightenment. Their particular approach was condemned by Pius X.

MYTH, in theological language, is a figurative overlay applied to persons or events in an effort to make their significance clearer. The term does not, therefore, denote falsity or fiction.

ORTHODOX (lit. 'having correct beliefs') is the name applied to Eastern Christians who are not in union with the patriarch of the Western, Roman, see.

PASCHAL is the adjective for the celebration of Easter, the Christian Passover (Heb. *Pesach*). The PASCHAL MYSTERY is therefore the great reality which is Jesus' death, resurrection, exaltation.

PATRIARCHAL: dealing with the founding fathers, the PATRIARCHS, and the biblical narratives that record their lives, beginning with Abraham.

PATRISTIC theology and literature come from the Fathers (Lat. *pater*), those great spokesmen in the first eight centuries of the Christian Church, East and West.

PAULINE literature is that attributed to the apostle Paul; those letters that can be more closely associated with his own literary activity are called PROTO-PAULINE, others less closely associated DEUTERO-PAULINE.

REALISED ESCHATOLOGY is a term given to an understanding of Jesus' message (e.g. in his parables) as suggesting it had already taken effect here and now, not merely in the future.

SAPIENTIAL is the adjective for the Wisdom (Lat. *sapientia*) literature (e.g. of the Bible).

SECULARISATION is the process of recognising the true character of secular, this-worldly realities, as distinct from SECULARISM, which denies the existence of any supernatural realities at all.

SYNOD (Grk 'coming together, meeting') is an assembly of a diocese or the whole Church. Since Vatican II there has been a Synod of Bishops in Rome every three years.

SYNOPTIC (Grk 'looking together') is the name applied to the Gospels of Matthew, Mark and Luke, who have a similar viewpoint on the life and ministry of Jesus by comparison with John.

TEMPORAL, of this time (Lat. *tempus*), as distinct from eternal, is a word applied to this-worldly realities.

TRADITION (Lat. *tradere*, 'hand on') is the process by which the community hands on—through scripture, in worship, by teaching, in catechesis, etc.—its basic experiences.

TRANSCENDENCE, as distinct from immanence, is that divine attribute by which God surpasses all human categories.

TYPOLOGY is an approach to interpreting the Old Testament, for example, by which some person or event is seen as a type (Grk *typos*, 'imprint, outline') of some future reality (anti-type).

WISDOM is a perspective that characterises certain books of the Bible, for example. One such book is actually called *Wisdom* (*of Solomon*).

BIBLICAL INDEX

GENERAL INDEX